SIMPLE BLESSINGS

14 Quilts to Grace Your Home

KIM DIEHL

Martingale®
& COMPANY

Simple Blessings:
14 Quilts to Grace Your Home
© 2004 by Kim Diehl

That Patchwork Place® is an imprint of
Martingale & Company®.

Martingale & Company
20205 144th Avenue NE
Woodinville, WA 98072-8478 USA
www.martingale-pub.com

MISSION STATEMENT

Dedicated to providing quality products and service to inspire creativity.

CREDITS

President ~ NANCY J. MARTIN

CEO ~ DANIEL J. MARTIN

Publisher ~ JANE HAMADA

Editorial Director ~ MARY V. GREEN

Managing Editor ~ TINA COOK

Technical Editor ~ CYNDI HERSHEY

Copy Editor ~ ELLEN BALSTAD

Design Director ~ STAN GREEN

Illustrator ~ BRIAN METZ

Cover and Interior Designer ~ STAN GREEN

Photographer ~ BRENT KANE

Printed in China
09 08 07 06 05 04   8 7 6 5 4 3 2 1

Library of Congress Cataloging-in-Publication Data

Diehl, Kim.
    Simple blessings : 14 quilts to grace your home / Kim Diehl.
        p. cm.
    ISBN 1-56477-519-4
    1. Patchwork—Patterns. 2. Quilting—Patterns. 3. Appliqué—Patterns. I. Title.
    TT835.D525 2004
    746.46'041—dc22
                                              2003021716

DEDICATION

For my family. Thank you for understanding my love of cutting up perfectly good fabric and then sewing it all back together again.

ACKNOWLEDGMENTS

A big thank you to Darlene Bott, Delene Kohler, Deslynn Mecham, and Terry Anderson for their willingness to give of their time and for their impeccable workmanship.

Special thanks to Celeste Freiberg and, most especially, Kathy Ockerman, for their beautiful machine quilting and cheerful smiles.

Heartfelt thanks to Michelle Price for the use of her wonderful home, which is so inviting and full of charm.

A round of applause for Tammy Peterson, who not only offered her piecing skills but bound more quilts for this book than I could count. A true-blue friend!

CONTENTS

THE PROJECTS

INTRODUCTION

I DIDN'T PLAN TO BECOME A QUILTMAKER, but somehow fate intervened and quiltmaking found me. While wandering through a sidewalk sale one afternoon, I chanced upon a sampler quilt pattern and was immediately smitten! Without hesitation, I impulsively purchased yards and yards of fabric, assorted sewing notions, and something called a rotary cutter. I dove headfirst into my new project, not knowing enough to be afraid, and learned each new step as I tackled it. After piecing my quilt top and working diligently to hand quilt it, I experienced an overwhelming feeling of satisfaction and pure elation as I sewed my last stitch. I was hooked!

Several years have passed since that sidewalk sale, and quiltmaking continues to be a source of pleasure in my life. I am particularly happy to be able to share some of my quilts with you, as well as my method of machine appliqué. This method very closely resembles the look of traditional hand appliqué, but you can use your sewing machine to accomplish it in much less time.

As a self-taught quilter, I never formally learned the rules pertaining to color but instead have learned to please myself and trust my instincts. Many of my quilts have a bit of the "make do" look and feature scrappy color schemes, but the fabrics and colors are chosen quite deliberately. This look is very simple to achieve and can be applied to any color scheme. I hope that you'll combine this method along with your own creative instincts to develop a style that is uniquely yours.

Most importantly, remember to enjoy your quiltmaking and don't worry about perfection! Whether you are a novice or an experienced quiltmaker, you'll see your skills improve with each completed project.

Display your quilts throughout your home and notice how they instantly lend an air of inviting warmth and charm to each room. Be creative! The projects presented in this book are versatile, and many can be made using rescued remnants from your scrap basket—so don't hold back. Mix and match to your heart's content and enjoy the fruits of your labor!

FABRIC SELECTION AND PREPARATION

IN THE FOLLOWING SECTIONS, you'll learn some basic tips for selecting quiltmaking fabrics and choosing project color schemes. The advantages and disadvantages of prewashing your fabrics before you begin a project are also discussed.

FABRICS FOR QUILTMAKING

Each project in this book is made from 100% cotton fabrics of high quality. I use cotton because it retains a crease when pressed, is easily manipulated for appliqué purposes, and is soft and lightweight for quilting.

PREWASHING FABRICS

Prewashing your fabric will remove the sizing and leave the cloth soft and easy to handle. Washing will also shrink the fabric slightly and remove any excess dye. On the other hand, many quilters prefer not to prewash fabrics because they enjoy the firmer texture and the little bit of oomph that the sizing lends. Fabrics that have not been prewashed will provide a softly puckered, vintage look when layered with cotton batting and backing, and then quilted and immersed in water.

If you choose to prewash your fabrics, place them in your washing machine on a warm setting with mild detergent. Dry your fabrics in a dryer on a medium setting until barely damp, and then press with a hot iron to remove any wrinkles.

If you decide not to prewash, dark-hued fabrics that pose a risk of bleeding (such as deep reds) should be tested to determine if they are colorfast. One method is to place a fabric swatch in a bowl of very hot water with a drop of detergent. After several minutes, remove the swatch and place it on two or three layers of white paper towel or muslin to dry. While the fabric is still wet, blot it with the paper towel to see if there is any transfer of color. After the swatch is dry, check the paper towel for any color residue. If you discover a loss of dye during any step of this process, use different fabric.

SELECTING COLOR SCHEMES AND PRINTS

The individual project directions in this book provide color choices that will duplicate the look of each featured quilt, but I encourage you to experiment and personalize your choices.

If you are new to quiltmaking, take time to look at quilts in books, magazines, and quilt shows. When you see something you like, study it and try to isolate what it is that pleases you. Are the colors low contrast or highly defined? Does the size and scale of the prints differ or do they read similarly? Do you find yourself drawn to tidy geometrics or do romantic florals make your heart flutter? As you become more attuned to your likes and dislikes, you will find that it becomes easier to make your fabric selections.

Through trial and error, I have developed the following guidelines for selecting fabrics for my own quilts:

- For a more traditional or formal look, choose fewer colors and repeat them throughout the top. One print will usually be used for each color.

- For just a bit of the "make do" look, first select the prints that will make up your main color scheme, and then add several look-alikes. In other words, choose fabrics with similar hues and scale of print to imply that you ran short of your main selections and had to substitute others. This method will make you successful if you're having a difficult time choosing one perfect print.

- To achieve a planned scrappy look, select your colors and prints as you would for a "make do" quilt. Then add several lighter, brighter, and darker shades, along with a few complementary colors. Vary the size and scale of your prints for added interest. Your choices should appear deliberate.

- For a completely scrappy look, take the above guidelines one step further by throwing in colors and prints that are slightly off, but not glaringly so. Don't feel compelled to use the neon green frog print if you really don't like it; life's too short! You can give a sense of balance to these quilts by squinting your eyes and viewing the center to determine a predominant color.

Feature that color in your border for a balanced, pulled together look, or use it alone to calm a boisterous center. If your pattern is becoming lost in a sea of scraps, consider limiting your background prints or try using just one!

The above guidelines can be incorporated into nearly any quilt and can provide you with endless possibilities. Learn to please yourself and trust your instincts! I follow one simple rule when selecting my fabrics, and it has never failed me: When it's right, you'll know it instantly. If you're not sure it's right, you need to make changes!

Pin Point

For scrap quilts, cut a few extra patchwork pieces in each required size. This will allow you to make substitutions easily if you are less than pleased with the balance of color.

PATCHWORK PRINCIPLES

AMONG THE TOPICS included in this section are basic supplies you'll need to construct a quilt, as well as the specific techniques and procedures used to piece and assemble the featured projects. You'll notice that some steps are universally practiced, while others are unique and the result of my being a self-taught quilter. I encourage you to read through these steps and to incorporate them into your own quiltmaking routines.

STANDARD QUILTMAKING SUPPLIES

The following items are always within easy reach in my sewing room:

- ACRYLIC RULER: A ruler that is 18" in length with a 3" or 6" width and has clearly marked ⅛" increments will accommodate most projects. I also keep a 15" square ruler for mitering corners and trimming borders.
- BIAS TAPE MAKER: A tool that produces 1"-wide double-fold bias tape
- FRAYCHECK: A liquid seam sealant that prevents fabric edges from fraying
- IRON: An iron with a smooth, nonstick surface that is lightweight
- IRONING BOARD: Any board with a snug cover and a flat, nonpuffy pad
- MASKING TAPE: Quilter's ¼"-wide masking tape, as well as various other widths for hand quilting
- NEEDLES: A variety of sizes for your sewing machine, as well as for hand sewing. I sew with a size 80/12 needle on quilting-weight cottons.
- PENCILS: Mechanical pencils with 0.5 mm lead for drawing fine, crisp lines. Mark dark fabrics with a quilter's silver pencil.
- PINS: Glass-head pins or silk pins with a fine, thin shank

- ROTARY CUTTER AND MAT: A rotary cutter with a sharp blade and a mat specifically designed for cutting
- SCISSORS: A sharp pair of good-quality scissors for cutting fabric, and an inexpensive pair of medium-sized scissors for cutting paper and plastic
- SEAM RIPPER: Any design that fits comfortably in your hand
- SPRAY STARCH: Any brand for stabilizing limp fabric and blocking patchwork
- THREAD: High-quality thread in khaki and gray will accommodate most projects
- WATER-SOLUBLE MARKERS: Fine tipped, for marking fabric

YARDAGE AND PIECING REQUIREMENTS

The project directions in this book are based on 42"-wide fabric and assume a 40" useable width after prewashing. To make the best use of your yardages, always cut the pieces in the order given. All patchwork should be sewn with right sides together unless you are instructed differently.

Pin Point

When you begin a new project, take a moment to wind three or four bobbins. You'll save time later!

ROTARY CUTTING

Unless otherwise instructed, cut all pieces on the straight of the grain. To speed the process when cutting a large number of pieces, I fold my fabric in half with the selvages together, and then in half once more. This results in four pieces with each cut. Of course, the size of your pieces will determine how many folds can be made. Fabric that is creased or badly wrinkled should be pressed to lie flat before cutting.

Place your folded fabric on the cutting mat with the fold aligned along a horizontal line of the marked grid. Make a vertical cut along one side of your fabric to establish a straight edge. Begin cutting your pieces, measuring from this edge.

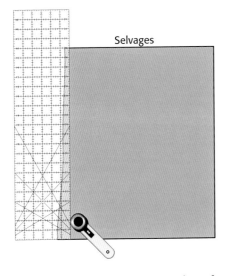

Selvages

To cut half-square triangles from squares, place the square (or layered stack of squares) on your cutting mat. Lay your ruler diagonally over the square with the cutting edge aligned directly over the corners and make the cut.

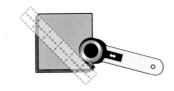

PINNING

As a personal preference, I pin my layered patchwork pieces together before feeding them through the sewing machine. It is a good practice to place pins at even intervals, including each sewn seam and intersection. I don't pin my pieces at the front edge where they feed under the presser foot because the presser foot holds them in place. However, I always pin the tail end of my layered patchwork because the back edge will often fishtail, which can cause an inaccurate seam allowance. If you pin this edge, you can lay your finger over the pin head and use it to steer the patchwork through the machine in a straight line.

As I stitch toward a pin, I generally don't remove it but instead greatly reduce my speed just as the needle passes over it. Slowing my speed allows the needle to slide over the pin, as opposed to high-speed sewing, which often results in the needle striking the pin and breaking. Ultimately, you should experiment to determine a method of pinning that works well for you and accommodates your sewing machine.

MACHINE PIECING

Unless instructed differently, always remember to join your fabrics with right sides together. Never estimate the width of the seam allowance as you stitch, because successful machine piecing requires that you produce consistent and accurate ¼" seams. If your seam allowance is off by as

As you begin sewing a machine-stitched seam, grasp the spool and bobbin threads and pull them gently as the fabric begins to feed under the presser foot. This will enable the fabric to feed smoothly and will also prevent thread snarls.

Re-evaluate the quality of your sewn seams periodically. Proper tension and stitch settings will provide stitches that remain invisible, even after the seams are pressed open.

little as $1/16$", this difference will multiply with each seam sewn and can result in finished blocks or entire pieced units that don't fit together. Here are two methods to help you achieve accuracy:

- Use a $1/4$" presser foot made specifically for quiltmaking.
- Make a visual guide by gently lowering the needle of your sewing machine until the point rests upon the $1/4$" line of an acrylic ruler. Ensure that the ruler is aligned in a straight position and apply a line of masking tape to the sewing-machine surface exactly along the ruler's edge, taking care not to cover the feed dogs. Align the edge of your fabrics with this taped line when feeding them through the machine.

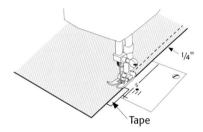

It is a good idea to check the accuracy of your seam allowance from time to time. This can be done as follows:

1. Cut three rectangles of fabric measuring $1\frac{1}{2}$" x 3", and sew them together side by side along the long edges; press the seam allowances in one direction.

2. The width of the center rectangle should measure 1". If it does not, make adjustments.

TEST BLOCKS

Before piecing a quilt with complex or small-scale blocks, you may wish to make a test block. After the block is complete, measure its size for accuracy and make any necessary adjustments. This will save lots of time and frustration later.

STRIP PIECING

To simplify the piecing process for patchwork with repeated patterns, such as checkerboard, lengths of fabric can be sewn together into strip sets. I prefer to press the seam allowance of each new strip as it is added to a set, usually toward the darker fabric, unless instructed differently. After each strip set is pressed, it should be placed squarely on the cutting mat and cut at measured intervals through the seams to create a strip-set segment. Align a horizontal line on your ruler with a seam line to square up the beginning of the set as well as to make subsequent cuts.

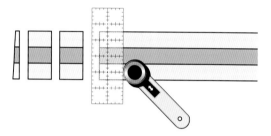

Strip piecing will save an enormous amount of time and eliminate some of the steps that would be required to stitch individual pieces together one by one.

CHAIN PIECING

When you begin a project that requires you to join numerous identical pieces, chain piecing will speed the process and save a good deal of thread. Chain piecing simply means that you continue to feed pieces through your sewing machine one after another, without snipping the threads between each. After all the pieces have been sewn, cut the threads to separate them and press as instructed.

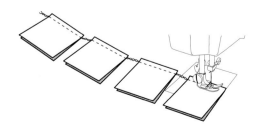

Pressing Seams

It is important to press your patchwork well so that the blocks fit together and lie flat when pieced into a quilt top. I use an iron that has been set on a hot, dry setting to press my pieces as follows:

1. Lay the patchwork on the ironing board with the fabric you wish to press toward (the fabric is usually dark) positioned on top. On the wrong side of the fabric, briefly bring the iron down onto the closed seam.

2. Lift the iron and fold the top piece of fabric back to expose the seam. While the fabric is still warm, run your fingernail along the sewn thread line to relax the fibers at the fold.

3. Press the seam flat from the front. The seam allowance will now lie under the fabric that was originally positioned on top.

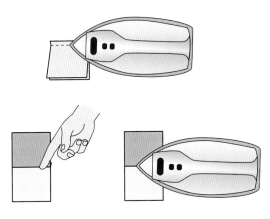

This method will help you achieve a finished block of accurate size, since less fabric is lost to the pressed fold of the seam allowance.

Pressing Triangle Units

Here is another quick but important pressing tip that works beautifully for me. Several patterns in this book instruct you to create triangles by layering a square with a drawn diagonal line on top of a second piece of cut fabric—another square or rectangle. After layering, the pair is stitched together on the drawn line and pressed. I recommend that these triangle units be pressed as follows:

1. After stitching, open the sewn triangle and align its corner to the corner of the bottom piece of fabric to keep it square. Press in place.

2. Trim away the excess layers of fabric under the top triangle, leaving a ¼" seam allowance.

Common practice is to trim away the excess layers first and then press, but I have found that for smaller scale patchwork in particular, the pressing method outlined above is very reliable and results in fewer blocks that require squaring up later.

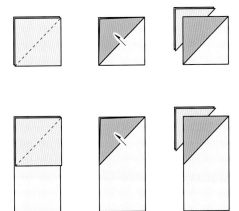

Completing the Quilt Top

THE FOLLOWING SECTIONS will guide you through the various steps needed to turn your beautiful blocks into a spectacular quilt. From block placement to mitered borders, it's all here!

Quilt-Top Assembly

It is always a good practice to square up your blocks prior to assembling them into a quilt top. If blocks are too small, double-check the seam allowance widths for accuracy. Check your pressing to ensure that no excess fabric has been lost in the folds along the pressed seam lines. Slightly trim outer edges on blocks that are too large. Distorted or misshapen blocks can be lightly spritzed with spray starch, reshaped, and pressed into place.

Lay out the blocks and evaluate the balance of color, repositioning as necessary or even making substitutions to achieve the final look that you desire. To keep your blocks in their proper positions during assembly, use small adhesive stickers or a water-soluble marker to lightly number each one on the wrong side. I number from left to right with the row and block number. For example: 1-1, 1-2, 1-3 and 2-1, 2-2, and 2-3.

Normally, the seams of each row will be pressed in alternating directions so that they butt together when joined. For greater ease when assembling large tops, join the rows in groups of two or three. Next, join the grouped rows, working from each opposite end toward the middle, until you join the two halves.

Pin Points
When arranging your blocks for placement into a quilt top, always position pieces with strong hues in the corners. This will clearly define and anchor your quilt center.

When you are joining large blocks or adding border strips to a quilt top, find the center of each and finger-press a crease. Line up the creases and pin in place for a perfect fit!

Borders

Please note that *pieced* borders may require extra attention to accuracy to ensure that they fit the quilt center properly. Borders that are too long can appear ruffled, while borders that are too small can cause puckered areas in the quilt center.

All of the border measurements in this book are mathematically correct, but you may wish to adjust the length of *whole cloth* border strips to allow for personal sewing differences.

Mitered Borders

The pattern measurements for mitered border strips include extra length to allow for the placement of the miters.

1. Find the center of the border strip and with right sides together, align it with the midpoint of the quilt top; pin in place, with the excess border fabric extending beyond the quilt top edges. Stitch the border to the quilt top, starting and stopping ¼" from each corner and backstitching. Repeat with the remaining borders.

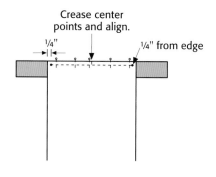

Crease center points and align.

¼"   ¼" from edge

2. With the wrong side up, lay the quilt top flat and overlap the border strips at one corner so that they cross at a 90° angle. Place a large acrylic ruler containing a 45°-angle line over the strips, positioning it so that the 45° line is aligned with the edge of the border and the ruler's edge intersects the corner seam. Use a mechanical pencil to draw a line along the ruler edge where it lies across the border. Now place the bottom border strip on top and repeat the process. Prepare each corner in this manner.

3. With right sides together, fold the quilt top and align the strips at one corner. Place pins through the drawn miter lines of both strips to align them perfectly. Beginning at the inside corner, backstitch and sew the strips together exactly on the drawn lines to the outside edges. Lay the top down to check that the mitered seam lies flat. Trim away the excess fabric, leaving a ¼" seam allowance. Press the seam open. Repeat with the remaining corners.

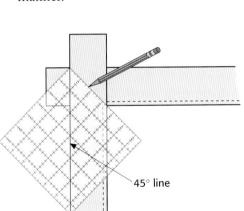

45° line

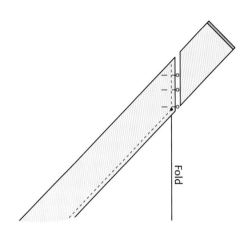

Fold

Finishing Techniques

In the sections that follow, I'll explain how your choice of batting can affect the appearance of your finished quilt, as well as the steps and techniques that I use when preparing projects for the quilting process. We'll also cover several styles of quilting, and I'll share the method I use for my own unique style of binding.

Batting

There are many types of batting available for a variety of looks. Polyester batting ensures minimal shrinkage when washed and can provide a more contemporary look. If you combine thin cotton batting with cotton fabrics that aren't prewashed, your quilt can take on a softly puckered, vintage look after being immersed in water. Experiment to determine your preferences and always follow the manufacturer's instructions provided on the batting package.

Pin Point
To easily thread a needle with a small eye, place a drop of Fraycheck near the end of your thread, smooth it between your fingers, and then allow it to dry. Several lengths can be prepared ahead and then wrapped around a piece of batting to prevent tangling.

Backing

I cut and seam my quilt backings to be 3" to 4" larger on all sides than the quilt top. When you choose your backing fabric, remember that busy-looking prints will make your quilting less visible, while muted prints and solids will emphasize your stitches and quilting design.

Basting

To prepare your top for the hand-quilting process, layer it with the batting and backing to form a quilt "sandwich," and then baste the layers together.

1. Place the backing fabric, wrong side up, on a large, flat surface. Smooth away any wrinkles and use masking tape to secure it in place.

2. Layer the batting over the secured backing fabric, centering it and smoothing away any wrinkles.

3. Center the quilt top over the first two layers and baste in place from corner to corner. Then baste vertically and horizontally at 3" to 4" intervals with a long needle and white thread.

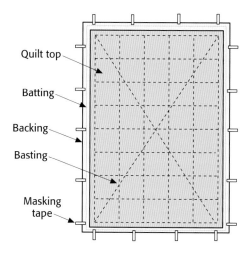

Quilt top
Batting
Backing
Basting
Masking tape

Marking Quilt Designs

Quilt tops can be marked in many ways, depending upon the look you wish to achieve and the style of your quilt. If your quilt features appliqués that will be outlined, or if you plan to stitch in the ditch (along the seam line), it may not be necessary to mark the quilting pattern. Depending upon your preference, patchwork can be marked for outline quilting using ¼" masking tape. Grids or cross-hatching can be stitched onto background areas using various widths of masking tape as a guide. If you choose to use tape, remember to remove it at the end of the day to prevent any adhesive residue from adhering to the fabric.

More elaborate designs should be marked onto the quilt top with a fine-tipped water-soluble marker before assembling the quilt sandwich. To ensure that the lines can be removed, always test your marker on a fabric swatch *before* using.

QUILTING

There are many quilting methods available for your projects. I personally love the look of hand quilting, but I don't always have the time needed to accomplish this for all of my projects. Frequently I have the background areas of my quilts machine quilted, with the appliqué and block areas that I wish to emphasize left open for hand quilting. At first glance the quilt has the appearance of being completely hand stitched, although the actual hand quilting was done without a large investment of time.

Above all, make sure your quilt is adequately quilted. After devoting the time and effort to assemble your quilt top, now is not the time to skimp! Beautiful quilting can elevate the status of even the simplest quilt, while the most striking quilt will suffer in appearance if the quilting is scant.

If you choose to machine quilt your quilt, please refer to *Machine Quilting Made Easy!* (That Patchwork Place, 1994) by Maurine Noble for detailed instructions.

If you choose to hand quilt your project, here are basic instructions. With your quilt in a hoop or a frame, follow these steps:

1. Tie a knot in the end of a length of quilting thread approximately 18" long and insert the needle into the quilt top about 1" away from where you wish to begin quilting.

2. Slide your needle through the batting and bring it up through the quilt top, gently tugging until the knot pops into the center of the quilt sandwich between the layers of fabric.

3. Make small, even stitches along the marked lines, taking care to stitch through all layers. Ideally, the distance between each stitch should be equal in length to that of your stitches. While you want to achieve tiny stitches, a consistent stitch size is most important.

4. As you near the end of your thread, make a knot about ⅛" from the quilt top and insert your needle, sliding it through the batting only. Bring the needle back up through the top, about 1" beyond your last stitch, tugging gently until the knot disappears below the cloth; carefully clip the thread.

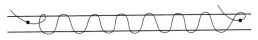
Hand-Quilting Stitch

Another charming style of hand quilting that I often use is the "big stitch" method. It can be accomplished with or without the use of a hoop and will provide you with swift progress, since a stitch length of ⅛" to ¼" is very acceptable. Simply use a #5 embroidery needle with #8 perle cotton to place a running stitch through the layers of the quilt sandwich. Begin and end your stitches as you would for traditional hand quilting.

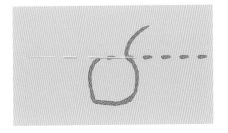

Pin Points

Try painter's low-stick masking tape when hand quilting. Many widths are available, the color is easy to see, and there is less chance of adhesive residue remaining on your top.

Run a thin line of Fraycheck around the perimeter of your quilt top before you begin the quilting process. This will prevent the edges from fraying and preserve your outer seam allowances!

Save the acrylic tubes that contain refill leads for your mechanical pencil and use them to store your needles. Adhesive labels can be placed on the tubes to identify the needle size.

BINDING

The quilts in this book are bound with one of two methods: the traditional 2½" French-fold method or a unique mock bias-tape method that I use for many of my own quilts. The pattern instructions provide yardage requirements for binding based on using 2½"-wide strips cut on the straight of the grain. The yardage will accommodate either method while providing enough binding to encircle the perimeter of the quilt plus approximately 10" extra to allow for corner pleats.

For traditional French-fold binding sewn from one single print, follow these steps:

1. With right sides together, join the 2½"-wide strips end to end at right angles, stitching diagonally across the corners, to make one long strip; trim the seam allowances to ¼" and press them open.

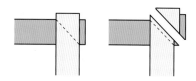

2. Cut one end at a 45° angle, turn it under ¼", and press in place. Fold the strip in half lengthwise with *wrong sides together* and press the center fold. If this quilt will include a hanging sleeve for display purposes, refer to "Making a Hanging Sleeve" on pages 19–20 and add it prior to binding the quilt. The binding will enclose the raw edges of the sleeve.

3. Beginning along one side of the quilt top, not a corner, use a ¼" seam to attach the binding, stitching along the raw edges. Stop sewing ¼" from the first corner and backstitch.

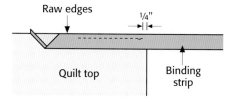

4. Make a fold in the binding, bringing it up and then back down onto itself to square the corner. Pivot the quilt 90° and reposition it under the presser foot. Resume sewing at the top edge of the quilt, continuing around the perimeter in this manner.

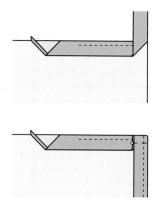

5. When you reach your starting point, cut the end at an angle 1" longer than needed and tuck it inside the sewn binding. Complete the stitching. The raw edges will be hidden within the binding.

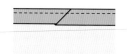

6. Bring the folded edge of the binding over to the back to cover the raw edges of the quilt. Use a blind stitch and

matching thread to sew the binding in place. At each corner, fold the binding to form a miter and stitch in place.

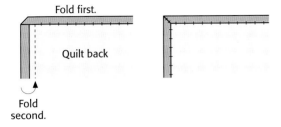

Fold first.

Quilt back

Fold second.

For the mock bias-tape method, follow these steps:

1. Cut and join 2"-wide strips as instructed previously in step 1 on page 18.

2. Slide the pieced strip through a bias-tape maker designed to produce 1"-wide, double-fold tape, pressing the folds with a hot iron as they emerge from the tape maker.

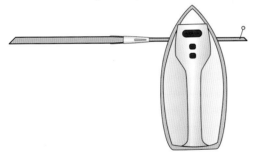

3. Open the fold of the strip along the top edge. Cut the beginning raw end at a 45° angle, turn it under ¼", and press in place. Starting along one side of the quilt top, not at a corner, align the unfolded raw edge of the binding tape with the raw edge of the quilt, and stitch as previously instructed in steps 3 and 4 on page 18.

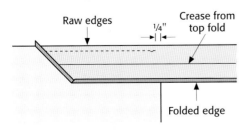

Raw edges

Crease from top fold

¼"

Folded edge

4. When you reach your starting point, cut the end 1" longer than needed and tuck it inside the sewn binding. Complete the stitching. The raw edges will be hidden within the binding.

5. Bring the folded edge of binding over to the back and hand stitch in place as instructed in step 6 of French-fold method.

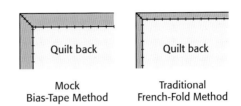

Quilt back

Quilt back

Mock Bias-Tape Method

Traditional French-Fold Method

The mock bias-tape method of binding will result in a traditional look for the front of your quilt, while producing a wider binding on the back and providing extra color to frame the backing beautifully.

For a scrappy binding that is pieced from assorted lengths of varying prints, join the strips together end to end without the use of a diagonal seam. Then bind the quilt as instructed above, starting with a straight rather than diagonal fold at the beginning.

MAKING A HANGING SLEEVE

A hanging sleeve will provide the most efficient way of displaying your quilt on a wall, and it can be made from leftover quilt fabrics or muslin. It is attached as the binding is sewn to the quilt.

1. Cut a strip 8" wide and about 2" shorter than the width of your quilt. Fold the short ends under twice, measuring ¼" with each fold, and stitch.

2. Fold the strip in half lengthwise with wrong sides together. Center and baste it to the back of the quilt, positioning the raw edges so that they are flush with

Pin Point
Keep a small basket in your sewing room for saving leftover lengths of binding. They can be spritzed with water, pressed, and joined to form a scrappy binding!

Pin Point

When you are signing quilt labels or signature blocks, first iron a piece of freezer paper to the wrong side of the fabric to stabilize it. Remove the paper after you complete the writing.

the top raw edge of the quilt. As the binding is stitched, the edges of the sleeve will become permanently attached.

3. After the binding has been stitched, blindstitch the bottom of the sleeve in place.

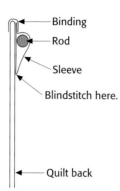

Binding
Rod
Sleeve
Blindstitch here.

Quilt back

ATTACH A QUILT LABEL

Remember to sign and date your quilt using a cloth label, and include any additional information you wish to share. Use a permanent, fine-tip marker to write on the label. Then hand stitch it to the back of your quilt.

MACHINE APPLIQUÉ MADE EASY

IN ADDITION TO the standard sewing supplies outlined in "Patchwork Principles" on page 10, you will need the following items:

- .004 MONOFILAMENT: Clear and smoke colors will accommodate any project
- BIAS BARS: Plastic or metal bars of various widths for use when making appliqué stems
- EMBROIDERY SCISSORS: A pair of small scissors with fine, sharp points for cutting cloth
- FABRIC GLUE STICK: Water-soluble and acid-free glue in stick form
- FREEZER PAPER: Any brand for use in making pattern templates
- IRON: A lightweight iron with a sharp pressing point, preferably with a non-stick surface, and/or a mini appliqué iron
- OPEN-TOE PRESSER FOOT: Allows for better visibility while stitching
- SEWING MACHINE: One with adequate tension control that is capable of producing a zigzag stitch
- SEWING-MACHINE NEEDLES: Fine, sharp, size 75/11 quilting needles
- STAPLE PULLER: A tool for removing staples from pattern templates
- STAPLER: A standard stapler for use when preparing pattern pieces
- TWEEZERS: A pair with rounded tips

PREPARING TO MACHINE APPLIQUÉ

When appliquéing by machine, you'll find that template and pattern piece preparation is every bit as important as the actual appliqué process itself. The sections that follow will guide you through these important steps, and I'll offer advice for utilizing your sewing machine to achieve truly invisible stitches.

Master Template Preparation

1. Use a mechanical pencil to trace the pattern onto the paper (nonwaxy) side of a piece of freezer paper. Place a second piece of freezer paper under the drawn pattern with the waxy sides together, and pin or staple in place.

2. Cut out the shape *exactly* on the drawn line and touch it with the tip of a hot iron to anchor the pieces together. Remove the pin or staples, and finish fusing the paper pieces together with the iron.

3. Mark any edge that does not need a seam allowance, such as a shape that is overlapped by another appliqué, with an *X*.

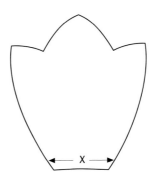

Pin Point

If you wish to appliqué a particular pattern but the shape appears too difficult, modify the pattern by fattening thin points and plumping narrow inner curves. No one will know it but you!

For smooth pattern-piece edges, move the paper as you cut, rather than the scissors. Producing a fluid shape is more important than achieving an exact replica of the pattern!

Keep a container of damp hand-wipes in your sewing room for easy cleanup when working with fabric glue.

To achieve consistent seam allowances when cutting appliqué pieces, place a small strip of ¼" masking tape on the end of your thumbnail to use as a visual guide.

Pattern-Piece Preparation

Paper pattern pieces should always be cut exactly on the drawn lines because the seam allowance will be added when the shapes are cut from fabric. As you prepare your pattern pieces, take care to achieve smooth edges because the shape you trace and cut will be the shape that graces your quilt!

1. Use the prepared template to trace the specified number of pattern pieces onto the paper side of a piece of freezer paper. To save time when many pieces are needed, stack the freezer paper four to six pieces deep. Then pin or staple, and cut several at once!

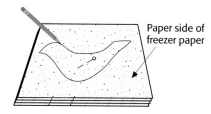

Paper side of freezer paper

2. Mirror-image pieces can easily be prepared by tracing the pattern onto one end of a strip of freezer paper, and then folding it accordion style before stapling and cutting. When you separate the pattern pieces, every other shape will be a mirror image.

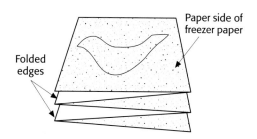

Paper side of freezer paper

Folded edges

Appliqué Preparation

1. Apply a small dab of glue from a fabric glue stick to the *paper* side of each pattern piece and affix it to the *wrong* side of your fabric, leaving approximately ½" between each shape. Position each shape with the longest lines or curves

on the diagonal, since bias edges are easier to manipulate than straight-grain edges.

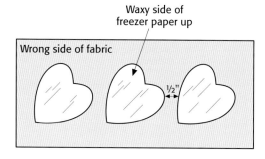

Waxy side of freezer paper up

Wrong side of fabric

½"

2. Cut out each shape, adding a scant ¼" seam allowance. Clip the seam allowance of all curves, both inner and outer, stopping a thread or two away from the edge of the paper. Smaller and more pronounced curves will need more clips while large, flowing curves will require fewer clips. Carefully clip inner points, such as the one you find at the top of a heart shape, right to the pattern-piece edge but not into the paper.

3. Working in a counter-clockwise direction, use the point of a hot, dry iron to press the seam allowance over onto the waxy side of the pattern piece, beginning at a straight or gently curved edge. Always press the seam allowance toward the center of the shape because puckers or pleats can form along the edge of your appliqué if the seam allowance lies at an angle. The point of a seam ripper can be used to help you grab and manipulate the fabric when you work with small appliqué shapes. Note that overly enthusiastic pressing

can cause the paper pattern piece edge to fold in upon itself and distort the shape of your appliqué, so take care!

NOTE: If you are left-handed, you should work in a clockwise direction.

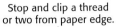
Stop and clip a thread or two from paper edge.

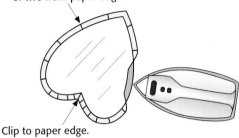
Clip to paper edge.

Preparing Outer Points

1. To prepare a sharp outer appliqué point, press the seam allowance so that the folded edge of the fabric extends beyond the first side of the pattern point.

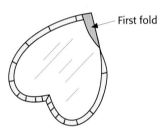
First fold

2. Fold over the seam allowance on the remaining side of the point and continue pressing. Apply a small amount of glue from the glue stick to the inside fold of cloth at the point (because fabric won't stick to fabric) and touch the cloth briefly with the point of a hot iron to fuse in place. Use embroidery scissors to carefully trim away any seam allowance fabric that extends beyond the point.

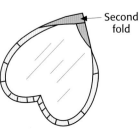
Second fold

Preparing Inner Points

Handle the fabric at inner points sparingly, because they can fray easily.

1. To prepare an inner point, fold the seam allowance leading up to the point over and onto the waxy side of the pattern piece. Follow with the point of a hot iron in a sweeping motion to fuse the fabric in place.

2. For the remaining side of the point, sweep the iron inward and away from the point to catch any stray threads while fusing the seam allowance fabric onto the waxy surface.

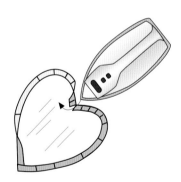

Evaluate the Prepared Appliqué

Always turn your prepared appliqué over to the front and evaluate your pressing and preparation. If you do discover a flaw along the prepared edge of the appliqué, simply loosen the seam allowance where it has occurred and re-press.

Background Fabric Preparation

1. To reduce fraying and protect the seam allowance of your background fabric, run a thin line of Fraycheck around the perimeter of each block or border.

2. Most of the appliqué patterns for blocks in this book utilize inner "valley" creases for placement guidelines to allow you to position your appliqués uniformly from block to block. With right sides together, fold the block in half and press a light crease along the center fold. Unfold the fabric, and then continue refolding and pressing to form vertical, horizontal, and diagonal creases.

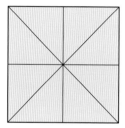

Sewing-Machine Preparation

1. Replace the needle of your sewing machine with a size 75/11 quilting needle and thread it with monofilament. Wind the bobbin with neutral-colored thread or thread to match your background fabric.

2. Program your sewing machine to the zigzag stitch and adjust the stitch width and length until you achieve a very small stitch, as shown above right. On my sewing machine, a width and length setting of one produces approximately twenty-six zigzag stitches to 1", measuring about $1/16$" wide—perfect! I also reduce the tension control to a level of one, as monofilament is very stretchy and if the tension is too tight, it can result in occasional bobbin threads becoming visible on the surface.

Approximate stitch size

3. If available for your machine, substitute an open-toe foot for your machine's standard presser foot to allow you to see your stitching easily as you sew.

MACHINE APPLIQUÉ METHODS

In the following sections, I'll cover the actual appliqué process and provide you with detailed "how-to" instructions for machine stitching your prepared appliqué pieces. With a little practice, you'll find that this technique is easily mastered. If time constraints or even just a plain fear of the unknown have made you hesitant to try appliqué projects, prepare to be surprised!

Invisible Machine Appliqué

1. Before you begin stitching, lay out all of the appliqué pieces on the background fabric to ensure that everything fits and is to your liking. You will always work from the bottom layer to the top, so remove all but the bottom appliqués and pin them in place, taking care not to place pins where you will be stitching.

2. Direct the needle and bobbin threads toward the back of the sewing machine and position the prepared block so that the needle will pierce the background fabric next to the appliqué when it is lowered. Place your fingertip over the monofilament while your machine takes two or three locking stitches or, if

your machine does not offer this feature, reduce the stitch length to the shortest setting and take two or three small stitches in place.

NOTE: The placement of the first zigzag stitch can vary depending upon your model of sewing machine. If your particular model is designed to drop the first stitch inside the appliqué, then position your fabric accordingly.

3. Lift your fingertip from the monofilament and begin zigzag stitching so that the "zig" stitches land a couple of threads inside the appliqué, and the "zag" stitches drop into the background fabric exactly next to the appliqué. After you stitch a short distance, pause and carefully clip the monofilament tail.

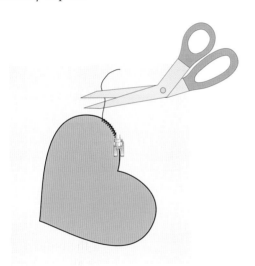

Stitch curved appliqué shapes at a slow to moderate speed to maintain a good level of control. Gently swivel the background fabric while you sew to keep the edge of the appliqué feeding straight toward the needle, or stop and pivot as often as needed to keep this angle of feed.

4. To secure an inner point or corner, stitch to the position where the inner zig stitch lands exactly on the inner point of the appliqué and stop. Pivot the background so that the appliqué inner point is at a right angle to the needle, and the next stitch will pierce the background. For sharp or narrow inner points, you may wish to pivot and stitch twice to secure the appliqué well. Make sure the appliqué edge is aligned properly under the presser foot and continue stitching.

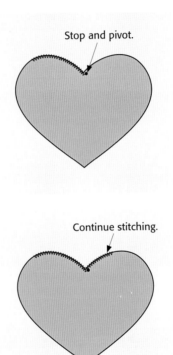

Stop and pivot.

Continue stitching.

5. To secure an outer point or corner, stitch to the position where the outer zag stitch lands exactly outside the appliqué point and pierces the background; then stop. Pivot the foundation so that the unsewn side of the appliqué is aligned to feed under the presser foot. As you continue sewing, a second stitch will drop into the point of the appliqué, securing it firmly to the background.

Stop and pivot.

Continue stitching.

6. Continue stitching around the perimeter of the appliqué until you are slightly beyond your starting position. End with a locking stitch, or take two or three straight stitches in place. Carefully clip all thread tails.

NOTE: You can choose to place your locking stitches within the appliqué or on the background. Position them where they will best be hidden.

String Appliqué

When there are two or more appliqués in close proximity, a method I call "string appliqué" will speed the process and reduce thread waste.

1. Stitch your first appliqué as instructed in the previous section "Invisible Machine Appliqué," but instead of clipping the threads when you finish, lift the presser foot and slide the background to the next appliqué without lifting it from the sewing-machine surface. Lower the presser foot and resume stitching, remembering to begin and end with a locking stitch.

2. Remove the background fabric from the sewing machine after the cluster of appliqués have been stitched, and carefully clip the threads between each.

REMOVE PAPER PATTERN PIECES

1. On the wrong side of the background fabric, use embroidery scissors to carefully pinch and cut through the fabric near the center of the appliqué shape. Do not puncture the freezer paper or you run the risk of cutting through your appliqué. Trim away the background fabric, leaving a generous ¼" seam allowance.

2. Grasp the appliqué between the thumb and forefinger of one hand, and the appliqué seam allowance with the thumb and forefinger of your other hand; give a gentle but firm tug and the edge of the freezer-paper pattern piece will come free. Use the tip of your finger or the point of a needle to loosen the remainder of the paper from the appliqué. Then peel it away and discard

the paper. If any paper remains in the appliqué corners, use a pair of tweezers to carefully remove it.

COMPLETE THE APPLIQUÉ PROCESS

1. Continue layering and stitching any additional appliqués until your block is complete. Keep in mind that you don't have to stitch any appliqué edges that are overlapped by another piece, and remember to remove the paper pattern pieces between each layer.

2. Place the completed block face down on your ironing board and lightly press from the back. Prolonged heat or high heat to the front of the block could weaken the monofilament and allow the appliqués to separate from the background fabric.

PRACTICE!

Before beginning your first project, I recommend experimenting with a couple of practice appliqués until you achieve the proper settings for your sewing machine and become comfortable with this technique. A heart-shaped practice pattern follows, since it provides gentle curves in addition to both inner and outer points.

I hope that you enjoy learning this fun and easily mastered method of appliqué!

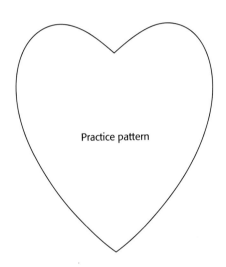

Practice pattern

COBBLESTONES AND CARTWHEELS

Scrappy blocks seem to cartwheel around a rich and colorful cobblestone center in this striking but simply pieced quilt.

Finished Quilt Size: 72½" x 72½"

MATERIALS FOR LAP QUILT

Yardages are based on 42"-wide fabric.
- 2⅝ yards of rusty orange print for borders and binding
- 2⅛ yards of cream print for background
- 2 yards of sage green print for borders
- 1 yard *total* of assorted prints for checkerboard
- 1 yard *total* of 16 assorted medium prints for blocks*
- ½ yard *total* of 16 assorted dark prints for blocks*
- Cranberry print scraps for border cornerstones
- Navy print scraps for border cornerstones
- 4½ yards of fabric for backing
- 78" x 78" square of batting

  * *You'll make 16 Cartwheel blocks using two prints—a medium and a dark—in the same color for each block.*

CUTTING

All strips are cut across the width of the fabric unless otherwise noted.

From the assorted prints for checkerboard, cut:
- 171 squares, 2½" x 2½"

From the cream print, cut:
- 15 strips, 2½" x 42"; crosscut into 234 squares, 2½" x 2½"
- 5 strips, 2⅞" x 42"; crosscut into 64 squares, 2⅞" x 2⅞". Cut each square in half diagonally to yield 128 half-square triangles.
- 9 strips, 1½" x 42"; crosscut into 128 squares, 1½" x 1½", and 64 rectangles, 1½" x 2½"

From *each* of the 16 assorted dark prints, cut:
- 5 squares, 2½" x 2½"
- 4 squares, 2⅞" x 2⅞"; cut each square in half diagonally to yield 8 half-square triangles

From *each* of the 16 assorted medium prints, cut:
- 4 rectangles, 2½" x 3½"

From the *lengthwise* grain of the sage green print, cut:
- 4 strips, 1½" x 50½"
- 4 strips, 2½" x 60½"

From the cranberry print scraps, cut:
- 4 squares, 1½" x 1½"
- 4 squares, 2½" x 2½"

From the *lengthwise* grain of the rusty orange print, cut:
- 4 strips, 2½" x 52½"
- 4 strips, 4½" x 64½"
- 4 strips, 2½" x 85"

From the navy print scraps, cut:
- 4 squares, 2½" x 2½"
- 4 squares, 4½" x 4½"

PIECE THE CENTER CHECKERBOARD UNIT

1. Lay out eight assorted print 2½" squares alternately with seven 2½" cream print squares to form a checkerboard strip; sew together. Press the seam allowances toward the assorted print squares. Repeat for a total of eight strips measuring 2½" x 30½".

2. Using eight 2½" cream squares and seven assorted print 2½" squares, repeat step 1. Repeat for a total of seven strips.

3. Lay out the checkerboard strips in alternating positions to form 15 horizontal rows; join the rows. Press all seam allowances in one direction. The center checkerboard unit should measure 30½" square.

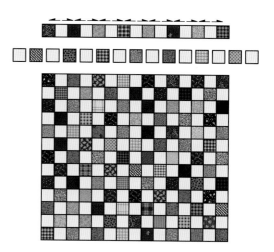

PIECE THE CARTWHEEL BLOCKS

The following instructions will yield *one* Cartwheel block. Remember to use the same dark and medium prints in each block. Repeat steps 1 through 7 for a total of 16 blocks.

1. With right sides together, layer a 2⅞" cream print triangle with a 2⅞" dark print triangle. Sew together, taking care not to stretch the bias edges. Press the seam allowances toward the dark print; trim away the dog-ear points. Repeat for a total of eight half-square-triangle units.

Make 8
per block.

Cobblestones and Cartwheels Lap Quilt

Finished Quilt Size: 72½" x 72½" • Finished Block Size: 10"

Designed by Kim Diehl and pieced by Tammy Peterson.
Machine quilted by Kathy Ockerman.

2. Lay out two 2½" half-square-triangle units, one 2½" cream print square, and one 2½" dark print square. Join the squares together. Press the seam allowances toward the whole squares. Repeat for a total of four corner units.

Make 4
per block.

3. Using a mechanical pencil, lightly draw a diagonal line on the reverse of each 1½" cream print square.

Pin Point

Try laying your fabric on a small rotary mat when marking sewing lines. The textured surface will grip your fabric, hold it in place, and prevent shifting.

4. With right sides together, layer a prepared 1½" cream print square over the corner on one end of a 2½" x 3½" medium print rectangle. Sew together exactly on the drawn line. Press and trim as instructed in "Pressing Triangle Units" on page 13. Repeat for a total of four pieced rectangles.

Make 4
per block.

5. Layer a prepared 1½" cream print square on the opposite corner of a pieced rectangle. Sew, press, and trim as instructed in step 4. Repeat for a total of four rectangle units.

Make 4
per block.

6. Join a 1½" x 2½" cream print rectangle to the pieced end of each rectangle unit from step 5. Press the seam allowance toward the cream rectangle. Repeat for a total of four pieced rectangle units.

Make 4
per block.

7. Lay out four corner units, four pieced rectangle units, and one 2½" dark print square to form a Cartwheel block. Sew the units together in each row. Press the seam allowances toward the dark print. Join the rows and press the seam allowances away from the center row. The pieced block should now measure 10½" square.

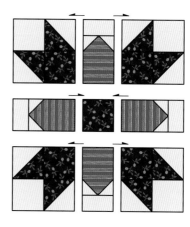

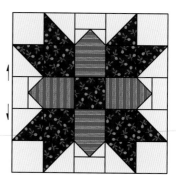

ASSEMBLE THE QUILT CENTER

1. Join three Cartwheel blocks end to end; press the seam allowances open. Repeat. Join these sections to opposite sides of the quilt center. Press the seam allowances toward the center.

2. Join and press five Cartwheel blocks as instructed in step 1. Repeat for a total of two strips. Join these strips to the remaining sides of the quilt. Press the seam allowances toward the quilt center. The pieced quilt top should now measure 50½" square.

PIECE AND ADD THE BORDERS

1. For border 1, sew a 1½" x 50½" sage strip to opposite sides of the quilt top. Press the seam allowances toward the border. Sew a 1½" cranberry square to each end of the remaining 50½" sage strips. Press the seam allowances toward the strips. Sew these pieced borders to remaining sides of the quilt top. Press the seam allowances toward the borders.

2. For border 2, sew a 2½" x 52½" rusty orange strip to opposite sides of the quilt top. Press the seam allowances toward the border. Sew a 2½" navy square to each end of the remaining 52½" rusty orange strips. Press the seam allowances toward the strips. Sew these pieced borders to the remaining sides of the quilt top. Press the seam allowances toward the borders.

3. For border 3, lay out fourteen 2½" cream print squares and fourteen assorted print 2½" squares to form a checkerboard strip. Join the squares. Press the seam allowances toward the assorted print squares. Repeat for a total of two strips. Sew these strips to opposite sides of the quilt top. Press the seam allowances toward border 2.

4. Repeat step 3 using fifteen 2½" cream print squares and fifteen assorted print 2½" squares. Sew these strips to the remaining sides of the quilt top and press the seam allowances toward border 2.

5. For border 4, refer to step 1 and use 2½" x 60½" sage strips and 2½" cranberry print squares.

6. For border 5, refer to step 1 and use 4½" x 64½" rusty orange strips and 4½" navy print squares.

COMPLETE THE QUILT

Refer to "Finishing Techniques" on pages 16–20 for details as needed. Layer the quilt top, batting, and backing. Quilt the layers together. The featured quilt was machine quilted with a meandering stipple pattern in the checkerboard center and an intersecting pattern of loops over the blocks. The borders feature feathered cables and elongated figure eights, with Xs quilted in the checkerboard strips. Use the four 2½" x 85" rusty orange print strips to bind the quilt.

PLEASANTLY PRIMITIVE

Softly muted shades of tan provide the backdrop for an exuberant tangle of patchwork blossoms in this charming wall hanging reminiscent of a primitive still-life painting.

Finished Wall-Hanging Size: 20½" x 34½"

MATERIALS FOR WALL HANGING

Yardages are based on 42"-wide fabric.

- ⅛ yard *each* of medium gold print and dark gold print for blocks and borders
- ⅛ yard *each* of medium rust print and dark rust print for blocks and borders
- ⅛ yard *each* of medium navy print and dark navy print for blocks and borders
- ⅛ yard *each* of medium blue print and dark blue print for blocks and borders
- ⅛ yard *each* of medium plum print and dark plum print for blocks and borders
- ⅛ yard *each* of medium burgundy print and dark burgundy print for blocks and borders
- ⅜ yard of medium tan print for inner border
- ¼ yard *each* of 4 coordinating light tan prints for background
- ¼ yard of dark tan print for outer border
- Fat quarter (or equivalent scraps) of green print for vines
- One 12" square of medium or dark plaid for vase appliqué
- Assorted green print scraps for blocks and leaf appliqués
- Scrap of medium print or solid for vase appliqué
- ⅞ yard of fabric for backing
- 26" x 40" piece of batting
- Water-erasable marker or mechanical pencil
- ⅜" bias bar

CUTTING

At first glance the cutting instructions for this project may seem lengthy but don't be intimidated! Each piece for the background is listed individually rather than in multiples because there are a variety of sizes that fit together like a puzzle. The process will go quickly!

To easily organize and piece the background portion of the quilt center, I divided it into six numbered sections and assigned a letter to the pieces within each section. As you cut each piece, use the water-erasable marker to lightly label the section number and letter on the reverse side. For example, use 1A, 2B, or 4E. I recommend that you keep the pieces within each section grouped together for easy assembly. Before you begin cutting, randomly assign a number from 1 to 4 to each ¼-yard cut of light tan print because the cutting instructions specify fabric 1, fabric 2, and so on.

All strips are cut across the width of the fabric unless otherwise noted. Refer to page 45 for the appliqué pattern pieces.

Cut the following pieces from the specified light tan prints:

Section 1
- 1A – 5½" x 7½" rectangle from fabric 1
- 1B – 2½" x 5½" rectangle from fabric 2
- 1C – 3½" x 4½" rectangle from fabric 3
- 1D – 3½" x 5½" rectangle from fabric 4

Section 2
- 2A – 5½" x 6½" rectangle from fabric 3
- 2B – 2½" x 5½" rectangle from fabric 1

Section 3
- 3A – 2½" x 2½" square from fabric 2
- 3B – 2½" x 3½" rectangle from fabric 3
- 3C – 1½" x 3½" rectangle from fabric 3
- 3D – 1½" x 3½" rectangle from fabric 3
- 3E – 2½" x 3½" rectangle from fabric 1
- 3F – 2½" x 2½" square from fabric 3
- 3G – 2½" x 2½" square from fabric 4
- 3H – 2½" x 5½" rectangle from fabric 1
- 3I – 3½" x 7½" rectangle from fabric 1

Section 4
- 4A – 2½" x 3½" rectangle from fabric 1
- 4B – 2½" x 3½" rectangle from fabric 4
- 4C – 1½" x 4½" rectangle from fabric 4
- 4D – 1½" x 3½" rectangle from fabric 4
- 4E – 3½" x 4½" rectangle from fabric 2
- 4F – 3½" x 7½" rectangle from fabric 2

Section 5
- 5A – 3½" x 4½" rectangle from fabric 4
- 5B – 1½" x 3½" rectangle from fabric 4
- 5C – 2½" x 4½" rectangle from fabric 4
- 5D – 2½" x 5½" rectangle from fabric 3
- 5E – 4½" x 5½" rectangle from fabric 2
- 5F – 2½" x 3½" rectangle from fabric 1
- 5G – 1½" x 3½" rectangle from fabric 1

Section 6
- 6A – 2½" x 3½" rectangle from fabric 2
- 6B – 3½" x 5½" rectangle from fabric 1
- 6C – 2½" x 3½" rectangle from fabric 1
- 6D – 3½" x 8½" rectangle from fabric 3

For the background portion of the Bear Paw Blocks, also cut from the light tan prints:
- 4 squares from fabric 1, 1⅞" x 1⅞"; crosscut each diagonally to yield 8 half-square triangles
- 2 squares from fabric 1, 1½" x 1½"
- 2 squares from fabric 2, 1⅞" x 1⅞"; crosscut each diagonally to yield 4 half-square triangles
- 1 square from fabric 2, 1½" x 1½"
- 2 squares from fabric 3, 1⅞" x 1⅞"; crosscut each diagonally to yield 4 half-square triangles
- 1 square from fabric 3, 1½" x 1½"
- 4 squares from fabric 4, 1⅞" x 1⅞"; crosscut each diagonally to yield 8 half-square triangles
- 2 squares from fabric 4, 1½" x 1½"

From *each* of the assorted medium prints (gold, rust, navy, blue, plum, burgundy), cut:
- 1 square, 2⅞" x 2⅞"; then crosscut it to yield 2 half-square triangles (you will only use 1 triangle)

Pleasantly Primitive Wall Hanging

Finished Wall-Hanging Size: 20½" x 34½" • Finished Block Size: 3"

Designed, pieced, machine appliquéd, and hand quilted in the big-stitch method by Kim Diehl.

From *each* of the assorted dark prints (gold, rust, navy, blue, plum, burgundy), cut:
- 2 squares, 1⅞" x 1⅞"; then crosscut each diagonally to yield 4 half-square triangles

Also from the assorted medium and dark gold, rust, navy, blue, plum, and burgundy prints, cut a combined total of:
- 15 squares, 2½" x 2½", for borders
- 15 squares, 1½" x 1½", for borders
- Random lengths of 2½"-wide prints to form a 120" length of binding when joined end to end

From the assorted green print scraps, cut:
- 3 squares, 2⅞" x 2⅞"; crosscut each diagonally for a total of 6 half-square triangles
- 15 pattern A pieces

From the 12" square of medium or dark plaid, cut:
- 1 pattern B piece

From the scraps of medium print or solid, cut:
- 1 pattern C piece
- 1 pattern C piece, reversed

From the fat quarter of green print, cut:
- Enough 1½"-wide bias strips to join into two 40" lengths when pieced end to end. (For added interest, each length can be pieced from a different green print or pieced from several prints.)

From the medium tan print, cut:
- 3 squares, 2½" x 2½"
- 2 rectangles, 2½" x 3½"
- 4 rectangles, 2½" x 4½"
- 4 rectangles, 2½" x 5½"
- 1 rectangle, 2½" x 6½"
- 1 rectangle, 2½" x 7½"
- 1 rectangle, 2½" x 9½"
- 1 rectangle, 2½" x 10½"
- 1 rectangle, 2½" x 12½"

From the dark tan print, cut:
- 6 squares, 1½" x 1½"
- 2 rectangles, 1½" x 2½"
- 1 rectangle, 1½" x 4½"
- 1 rectangle, 1½" x 5½"
- 1 rectangle, 1½" x 6½"
- 1 rectangle, 1½" x 7½"
- 1 rectangle, 1½" x 8½"
- 1 rectangle, 1½" x 10½"
- 1 rectangle, 1½" x 12½"
- 1 rectangle, 1½" x 13½"
- 1 rectangle, 1½" x 14½"

PIECE THE BEAR PAW BLOCKS

As you piece the Bear Paw blocks, please keep in mind that only one light tan print (fabric 1, 2, 3, or 4) is used for the background portion of each block. Piece the blocks as follows:

1. With right sides together, layer an assorted medium print 2⅞" triangle with a 2⅞" green print triangle. Sew the pair together along the long edge to form a 2½" half-square-triangle unit. Press the seam allowance toward the green print. Trim away the dog-ear points.

2. With right sides together, layer a 1⅞" assorted dark print triangle and a 1⅞" tan print triangle. Sew the pair together along the long edge to form a 1½" half-square-triangle unit. Press the seam allowance toward the dark print. Trim away the dog-ear points. Repeat for a total of four identical units.

3. Lay out the units formed in steps 1 and 2 along with one matching 1½" tan print square to form a Bear Paw block. Sew the pieces together. Press the seam allowances of the 1½" half-square-triangle units toward the tan print and the seam allowances of each row toward the center of the block.

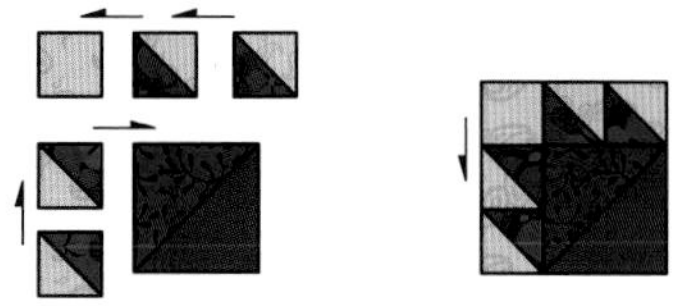

4. Repeat steps 1 through 3 to make a total of six Bear Paw blocks measuring 3½" square unfinished.

PIECE THE CENTER SECTIONS

For ease in assembly, the units within each section are pieced separately, and then the sections are joined. Insert Bear Paw blocks where indicated, matching block background to quilt background segments as best as possible. Lay out all sections first to be sure you are satisfied with the arrangement. Press the seam allowances of the joined pieces to one side, with the exception of the seams adjoining the Bear Paw blocks. These seams should be pressed toward the block whenever possible to simplify the appliqué process when the vines are added.

1. To make section 1, join segments 1A, 1B, 1C, and 1D.

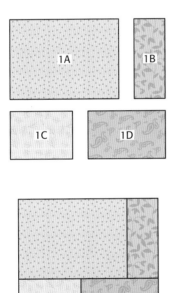

2. To make section 2, join segments 2A and 2B.

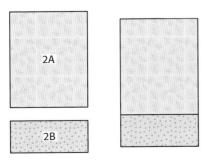

3. To make section 3, join segments 3A, 3B, 3C, 3D, 3E, 3F 3G, 3H, and 3I. Notice the placement of the Bear Paw block.

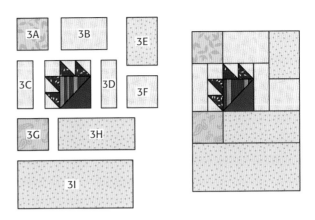

4. To make section 4, join segments 4A, 4B, 4C, 4D, 4E, and 4F. Notice the placement of the Bear Paw blocks.

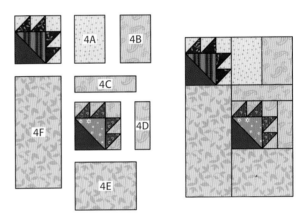

5. To make section 5, join segments 5A, 5B, 5C, 5D, 5E, 5F, and 5G. Notice the placement of the Bear Paw blocks.

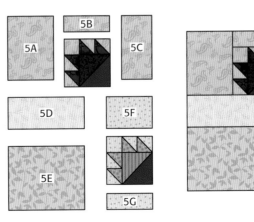

6. To make section 6, join segments 6A, 6B, 6C, and 6D. Notice the placement of the Bear Paw block.

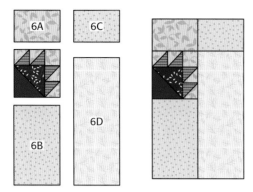

ASSEMBLE THE WALL-HANGING CENTER

1. Join the right side of section 1 to the left side of section 2 and press the seam allowance to one side.

2. Join the right side of section 3 to the left side of section 4 and press the seam allowance to one side.

3. Join the right side of section 5 to the left side of section 6 and press the seam allowance to one side.

4. Join the top edge of the section 1 and 2 unit to the bottom edge of the section 3 and 4 unit and press the seam allowance to one side.

5. Join the bottom edge of the section 5 and 6 unit to the top edge of the section 3 and 4 unit and press the seam allowance to one side. The pieced quilt center should now measure 14½" x 28½".

Appliqué the Wall-Hanging Center

Referring to "Machine Appliqué Made Easy" on pages 21–24, prepare the appliqués.

1. With *wrong* sides together, fold each 40"-long green strip in half lengthwise and stitch a scant ¼" in from the long raw edges to form a tube. Insert the bias bar into the tube and slide it along as you press the stem, making sure the seam is centered and lies flat.

Bias bar

2. Using the project photo as a guide and referring to "Invisible Machine Appliqué" on pages 24–26, lay out and stitch the vase appliqués. Take care to leave the top of the vase unstitched until the vines have been added so that their raw edges can be tucked underneath.

3. Beginning about ½" inside the green point of each Bear Paw block and working downward, lay out the vines, overlapping and weaving them among each other as though they were growing. Leave a small tail at the top of each vine for finishing the raw edge and use pins as needed to anchor the vines while you work.

4. At each place where the vine meets a Bear Paw block, cut the vine, leaving ½" for a seam allowance, and continue the vine if applicable on the other side of the block, again leaving a ½" seam allowance. Also, leave a ½" seam allowance where each vine meets the basket.

5. Use a fabric glue stick to affix the vines in place. The raw edges should be folded under about ¼" so that they rest upon the green points of the Bear Paw blocks. Appliqué the vines.

6. Lay out the fifteen prepared pattern A pieces in a random manner and appliqué them in place.

7. Appliqué the open area at the top of the vase appliqué.

Add the Inner Border

1. Lightly draw a diagonal line on the wrong side of a 2½" medium tan print square. With right sides together, layer it with an assorted print 2½" square. Sew together exactly on the drawn line. Press and trim as instructed in "Pressing Triangle Units" on page 13. Repeat for a total of three half-square-triangle units.

Make 3.

2. Set aside two 2½" x 5½" medium tan print rectangles and one 2½" x 4½" medium tan print rectangle. Lightly draw a diagonal line on the wrong side of fifteen assorted print 2½" squares. With right sides together, layer a prepared assorted print 2½" square on the end of each remaining 2½"-wide medium tan print rectangle and sew exactly on the drawn line. Press and trim as instructed in step 1 above.

NOTE: For steps 3 through 6, which use the medium tan print, the width of all segments is 2½". Therefore, only the length measurements are given. Always work from left to right when laying out the segments.

3. For the left inner border, lay out the following lengths of medium tan pieced segments from step 2: 12½", 3½", 9½", and 4½". Sew the segments together end to end. Press the seam allowances toward the medium tan print. Join this pieced border strip to the left side of the wall-hanging center. Press the seam allowance toward the wall-hanging center.

4. For the right inner border, lay out the following lengths of medium tan pieced segments from step 2: 4½" (this rectangle is not pieced), 4½", 10½", 6½", and two 2½" half-square-triangle units. Join the segments as instructed in step 3 and add the strip to the right side of the wall-hanging center. Press the seam allowance toward the wall-hanging center.

5. For the top inner border, lay out the following lengths of medium tan pieced segments from step 2: 5½" (this rectangle is not pieced), 2½" half-square-triangle unit, 7½", and 4½". Join the segments as instructed in step 3 and add the strip to the top of the wall hanging. Press the seam allowance toward the wall-hanging center.

6. For the bottom inner border, lay out the following lengths of medium tan pieced segments from step 2: 5½", 3½", 5½", and 5½" (this rectangle is not pieced). Join the segments as instructed in step 3 and add the strip to the bottom of the quilt center. Press the seam allowance toward the wall-hanging center.

Left Inner Border

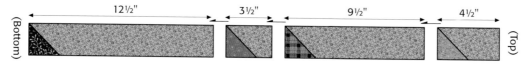

Join this edge to the quilt center, left side.

Right Inner Border

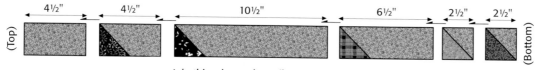

Join this edge to the quilt center, right side.

Top Inner Border

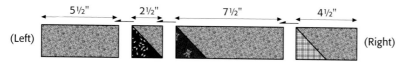

Join this edge to the quilt center, top.

Bottom Inner Border

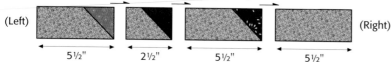

Join this edge to the quilt center, bottom.

ADD THE OUTER BORDER

For steps 1 through 4, which use the dark tan print, the width of all segments is 1½". Therefore, only the length measurements are given.

1. For the left outer border, lay out the following segments: 4½" tan print rectangle, assorted print 1½" square, 1½" tan print square, assorted print 1½" square, 1½" tan print square, assorted print 1½" square, 12½" tan print rectangle, assorted print 1½" square, and a 10½" tan print rectangle. Join the segments end to end; press the seam allowances toward the tan print. Sew this pieced strip to the left edge of the quilt top. Press the seam allowances away from the wall-hanging center.

2. For the right outer border, lay out the following segments: 1½" tan print square, assorted print 1½" square, 1½" tan print square, assorted print 1½" square, 13½" tan print rectangle, assorted print 1½" square, and a 14½" tan print rectangle.

Join the segments as instructed in step 1, and sew the strip to the right edge of the quilt top; press the seam allowances away from the quilt top.

3. For the top outer border, lay out the following segments: assorted print 1½" square, 1½" tan print square, assorted print 1½" square, 5½" tan print rectangle, assorted print 1½" square, 8½" tan print rectangle, assorted print 1½" square, and a 2½" tan print rectangle. Join the segments as instructed in step 1 and sew the strip to the top of the quilt.

4. For the bottom outer border, lay out the following segments: 2½" tan print rectangle, assorted print 1½" square, 6½" tan print rectangle, assorted print 1½" square, 7½" tan print rectangle, assorted print 1½" square, 1½" tan print rectangle, and an assorted print 1½" rectangle. Join the segments as instructed in step 1 and sew the strip to the bottom of the wall hanging. The pieced wall-hanging top should now measure 20½" x 34½".

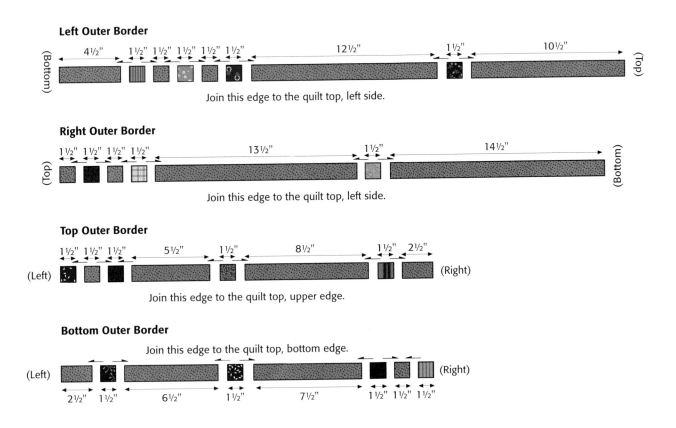

Left Outer Border

(Bottom) — 4½" — 1½" 1½" 1½" 1½" 1½" — 12½" — 1½" — 10½" — (Top)

Join this edge to the quilt top, left side.

Right Outer Border

(Top) — 1½" 1½" 1½" 1½" — 13½" — 1½" — 14½" — (Bottom)

Join this edge to the quilt top, left side.

Top Outer Border

(Left) — 1½" 1½" 1½" — 5½" — 1½" — 8½" — 1½" 2½" — (Right)

Join this edge to the quilt top, upper edge.

Bottom Outer Border

Join this edge to the quilt top, bottom edge.

(Left) — 2½" 1½" — 6½" — 1½" — 7½" — 1½" 1½" 1½" — (Right)

COMPLETE THE WALL HANGING

Refer to "Finishing Techniques" on pages 16–20 for details as needed. Layer the wall-hanging top, batting, and backing. Quilt the layers together. The featured wall hanging was hand quilted in the big-stitch method, with a background grid in the center section and the appliqués outlined for emphasis. Join the random 2½"-wide lengths of assorted prints to form a strip at least 120" in length and bind the wall hanging.

Appliqué Patterns

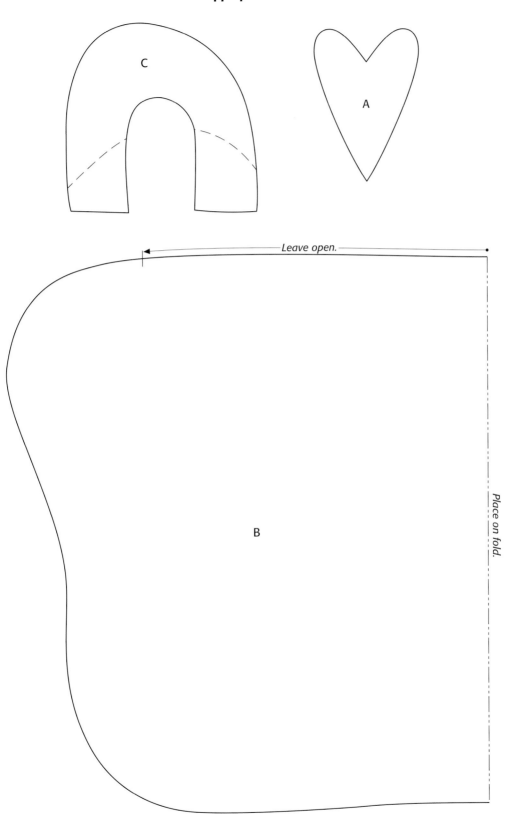

C

A

Leave open.

B

Place on fold.

GEESE IN THE GARDEN

Richly hued prints in cranberry, plum, gold, and green blend beautifully with a touch of blue to create a sun-dappled taste of autumn in this lap-sized quilt meant for snuggling.

Finished Quilt Size: 65½" x 65½"

MATERIALS FOR LAP QUILT

Yardages are based on 42"-wide fabric.
- 7½ yards of cream print for blocks, border, and binding
- 1⅛ yards of tan print for blocks
- ¾ yard of medium green print for vines
- Assorted print scraps in green, gold, dark brown, light brown, cranberry, plum, and blue for appliqués
- 4½ yards of fabric for backing
- 71" x 71" square of batting
- ⅜" bias bar

CUTTING

All strips are cut across the width of the fabric unless otherwise noted. Refer to page 53 for the appliqué pattern pieces.

From the tan print, cut:
- 5 strips, 2⅛" x 42"; crosscut into 82 squares, 2⅛" x 2⅛". Cut each square in half diagonally to yield 164 half-square triangles.
- 7 strips, 2⅞" x 42"; crosscut into 82 squares, 2⅞" x 2⅞". Cut each square in half diagonally to yield 164 half-square triangles.
- 3 strips, 1½" x 42"; crosscut into 41 squares, 1½" x 1½"

From the cream print, cut:
- 5 strips, 2⅛" x 42"; crosscut into 82 squares, 2⅛" x 2⅛". Cut each square in half diagonally to yield 164 half-square triangles.
- 18 strips, 1½" x 42"; crosscut into 164 squares, 1½" x 1½", and 164 rectangles, 1½" x 2½"
- 6 strips, 5½" x 42"; crosscut into 40 squares, 5½" x 5½"
- 8 strips, 2½" x 42"
- 4 strips, 10½" x 75", from the *lengthwise* grain of the fabric

From the assorted light brown prints, cut:
- 4 pattern A pieces

From the assorted gold prints, cut:
- 16 pattern B pieces

From the assorted dark brown prints, cut:
- 16 pattern C pieces

From the assorted cranberry prints, cut:
- 24 pattern D pieces
- 24 pattern E pieces (Keep in mind that the appliqués cut with pattern E are layered over the appliqués cut with pattern D, so select prints that contrast.)
- 70 pattern I pieces (You can cut more or less, depending on your preferences.)

From the assorted blue prints, cut:
- 4 pattern F pieces
- 8 pattern G pieces (Keep in mind that the appliqués cut with pattern G are layered over the appliqués cut with pattern F, so select prints that contrast.)

From the assorted green prints, cut:
- 50 pattern H pieces

From the assorted plum prints, cut:
- 120 pattern I pieces

Piece the Goose Track Blocks

1. With right sides together, layer a 2⅛" tan print triangle with a 2⅛" cream print triangle. Sew the triangles together along the long edge, taking care not to stretch the bias. Press the seam allowance toward the tan print. Trim away the dog-ear points. Repeat for a total of 164 half-square-triangle units.

2. Cut each half-square-triangle unit in half diagonally for a total of 328 tan-and-cream quarter-square-triangle pairs.

Cut apart for
328 pieced triangles.

3. Join the tan edge of a triangle pair from step 2 to a 1½" cream print square; press the seam allowance toward the cream print. Repeat for a total of 164 pieced units.

Make 164.

4. Join the tan edge of an additional triangle pair from step 2 to the adjacent edge of the 1½" cream print square. Press the seam allowance toward the cream print. Trim away the dog-ear points. Repeat for a total of 164 pieced triangle units.

Make 164.

5. Join a 2⅞" tan print triangle to the long edge of a pieced triangle unit from step 4. Press the seam allowances toward the tan print. Trim away the dog-ear points. Repeat for a total of 164 quarter-block units.

Make 164.

6. Join a 1½" x 2½" cream print rectangle to opposite sides of a 1½" tan print square. Press the seam allowances toward the cream print. Repeat for a total of 41 rectangle units.

Make 41.

7. Join a quarter-block unit from step 5 to each long side of the remaining 1½" x 2½" cream print rectangles so that they form a mirror image. Press the seam allowances toward the cream print. Make a total of 82 half-block sections.

Make 82.

8. Lay out the half-block sections from step 7 and one rectangle unit from step 6 in three horizontal rows to form a Goose Track block. Sew the rows together. Press the seam allowances toward the cream print. Repeat for a total of 41 blocks measuring 5½" square unfinished.

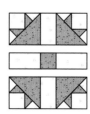 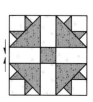

Make 41.

Geese in the Garden Lap Quilt

Finished Quilt Size: 65½" x 65½" • Finished Block Size: 5"

Designed, pieced, and machine appliquéd by Kim Diehl. Machine quilted by Kathy Ockerman.
Hand quilted accents by Kim Diehl.

Piece the Quilt Center

Lay out the Goose Track blocks and the 5½" cream print squares in alternating positions to form nine horizontal rows with each row containing nine blocks. Sew the blocks together in each row. Press the seam allowances toward the cream print squares. Then join the rows. Press the seam allowances toward the rows that begin and end with the cream print squares. The pieced quilt center should now measure 45½" square.

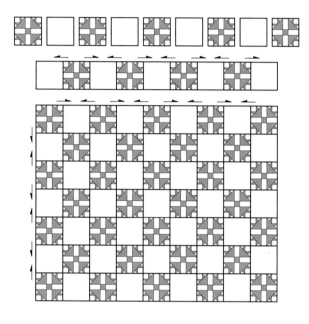

Pin Point

Whenever a pieced block or unit is joined to a whole piece of fabric of the same size, it is an opportunity to check the accuracy of your seam allowances. If there is a size discrepancy, check for errors and make corrections before continuing.

Appliqué the Borders

Referring to "Machine Appliqué Made Easy" on pages 21–24, prepare the appliqués.

1. Fold the ¾ yard of medium green print in half with the selvages together and press flat. Cut a 15" square, positioned on the bias, through both layers of fabric. If a 15" square doesn't fit perfectly across the width of the fabric, it's okay to slightly shift the angle of the square on the fabric. Reserve the green scraps for later use.

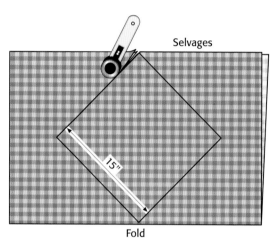

2. On the wrong side of each green square, use a mechanical pencil and ruler to lightly draw lines at 1¼" intervals. Align the drawn lines and pin in place with right sides together. Stitch together along the pinned edge and press the seam allowances open.

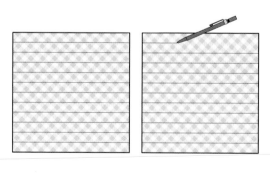

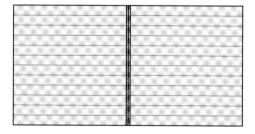

3. Align the drawn lines on the remaining raw edges, with the rows offset by one row; pin with right sides together to form a tube. Stitch together; press the seam allowance open. Use scissors or a rotary cutter to cut along the drawn lines for a continuous bias strip.

4. With wrong sides together, fold the bias strip together and use a scant ¼" seam allowance to stitch along the long raw edges to form a tube. Insert the bias bar into the tube and slide it along as you press the stem, making sure the seam is centered and lies flat.

5. Cut eight 36" lengths of prepared bias tube to be used for the vines. Set aside the remaining length for later use.

6. Fold a 10½" x 75" cream print border strip in half end to end to find the center; use a hot, dry iron to lightly press a crease to denote this position. Lay the pressed border strip along one edge of the pieced quilt center, with the center positions aligned. Use a safety pin to mark the position of the ends of the quilt center on the strip. Repeat with the remaining border strips.

7. Using the center crease and quilt photo for placement, lay a prepared vase and three pomegranate appliqués on a border strip. When you are pleased with their positions, pin the pomegranates in place and remove the vase. Referring to "Invisible Machine Appliqué" on pages 24–26, begin stitching the appliqués to the border strip. Repeat with the remaining border strips.

8. Cut the reserved length of vine into 6" segments. From the remaining scraps of medium green print, cut as many additional 1¼" x 6" bias strips needed to make a total of twenty-four 6" segments. Prepare the additional stems as instructed in step 4.

9. Referring to the quilt photo for placement, use the fabric glue stick to affix two 36" vines to each border strip, beginning at the center grouping of pomegranates and taking care not to work beyond the point of the safety pins. Add three 6" stems to the vine on each side of the pomegranates, tucking the raw edges under the vines.

10. Appliqué the vines and stems in place. Then add the remaining appliqués to each border strip, again taking care not to work beyond the point of the safety pins. Any appliqués that need to be positioned in the corners will be added after the border strips are joined to the quilt center.

ADD THE BORDERS AND COMPLETE THE APPLIQUÉ

Referring to "Mitered Borders" on pages 14–15, add the borders and miter each corner. Pin any unsewn vine lengths to the borders to prevent them from being caught in the miters. Appliqué the remaining pieces to each corner of the borders.

COMPLETE THE QUILT

Refer to "Finishing Techniques" on pages 16–20 for details as needed. Layer the quilt top, batting, and backing. Quilt the layers together. The featured quilt was machine quilted with a spiraling circle over the Goose Track blocks, and a design inspired by the leaf shapes was placed onto the cream setting squares. The appliqués in the border were echo quilted to emphasize their shapes. Use the eight 2½" x 42" cream print strips to bind the quilt.

Appliqué Patterns

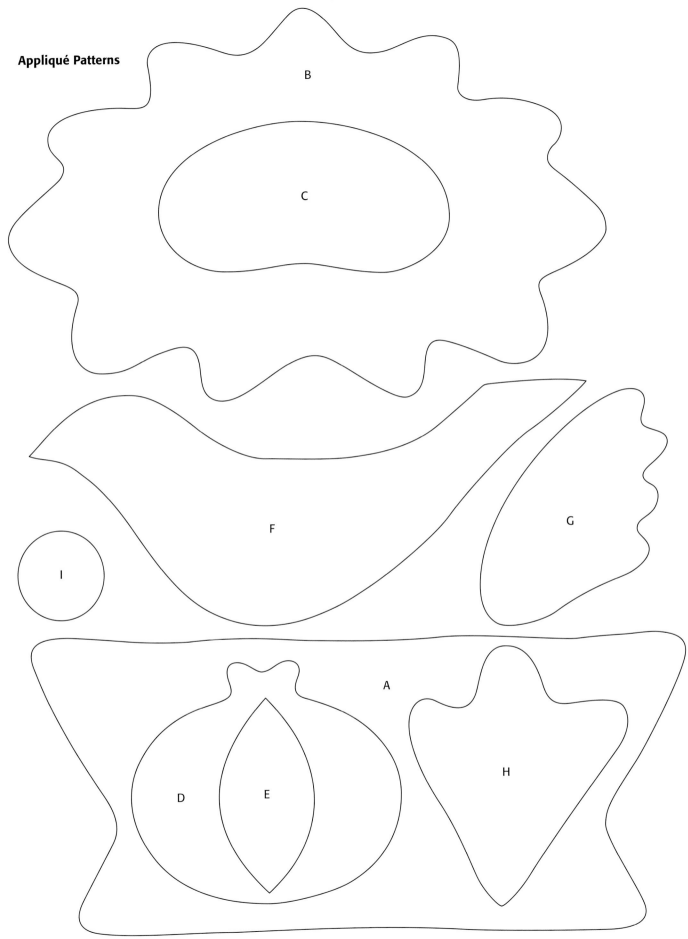

B

C

F

I

G

A

D

E

H

A Dash of Tradition

Long a favorite of quilters, the traditional Churn Dash block takes on a decidedly romantic feel when paired with lush red and cream prints. Strip-piecing techniques make the block and quilt-top assembly a snap!

Finished Quilt Size: 82½" x 93½"

Materials for Bed Quilt

Yardages are based on 42"-wide fabric.
- 8 yards of cream print for block background
- 6⅛ yards of dark red print for blocks and binding
- 1⅞ yards of medium red print for blocks
- 7½ yards of fabric for backing (3 widths pieced horizontally)
- 88" x 99" rectangle of batting

Cutting

All strips are cut across the width of the fabric unless otherwise noted.

From the cream print, cut:
- 50 strips, 1½" x 42"
- 8 strips, 4½" x 42"
- 1 strip, 5" x 42"
- 1 strip, 10½" x 42"
- 40 strips, 2⅞" x 42"; crosscut into 510 squares, 2⅞" x 2⅞"
- 18 strips, 1" x 42"; trim 4 strips to 39". Cut 9 strips into 60 rectangles, 1" x 5½". Cut 5 strips into 168 squares, 1" x 1".

From the dark red print, cut:
- 40 strips, 1½" x 42"
- 40 strips, 2⅞" x 42"; crosscut into 510 squares, 2⅞" x 2⅞"
- 10 strips, 2½" x 42"

From the medium red print, cut:
- 18 strips, 1" x 42"
- 26 strips, 1½" x 42"; crosscut into 672 squares, 1½" x 1½"

Prepare the Strip Sets

1. Join three 1½" x 42" cream print strips and two 1½" x 42" dark red print strips to form strip set 1. Press the seam allowances toward the red print. Repeat for a total of 10 sets. Cut each set into 1½" segments for a total of 255.

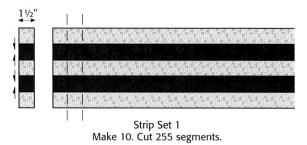

1½"

Strip Set 1
Make 10. Cut 255 segments.

2. Join one 1½" x 42" cream print strip and one 1½" x 42" dark red print strip to form strip set 2. Press the seam allowances toward the red print. Repeat for a total of 20 sets. Cut each set into 1½" segments for a total of 510.

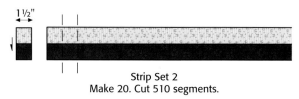

1½"

Strip Set 2
Make 20. Cut 510 segments.

3. Join one 4½" x 42" cream print strip between two 1" x 42" medium red print strips to form strip set 3. Press the seam allowances toward the red print. Repeat for a total of eight sets. Cut each set into 1" segments for a total of 310.

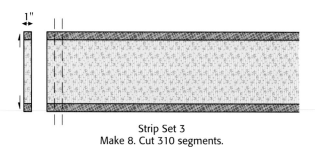

1"

Strip Set 3
Make 8. Cut 310 segments.

4. Join one 5" x 42" cream print strip and one 1" x 42" medium red print strip to form strip set 4. Press the seam allowance toward the red print. Cut the set into 1" segments for a total of 24.

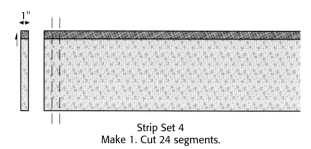

1"

Strip Set 4
Make 1. Cut 24 segments.

5. Join one 10½" x 42" cream print strip and one 1" x 42" medium red print strip to form strip set 5. Press the seam allowance toward the red print. Cut the set into 1" segments for a total of 28.

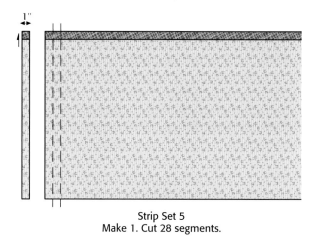

1"

Strip Set 5
Make 1. Cut 28 segments.

Piece the Churn Dash Blocks

1. Using a mechanical pencil, lightly draw a diagonal line on the wrong side of each 2⅞" cream print square.

Pin Point
To eliminate fraying or stretching as you draw sewing lines on fabric, begin marking at the center position and draw the lines out toward each opposite edge.

A Dash of Tradition Bed Quilt

Finished Quilt Size: 82½" x 93½" • Finished Block Size: 5"

Designed by Kim Diehl and pieced by Deslynn Mecham.
Machine quilted by Celeste Freiberg and Kathy Ockerman.

2. With right sides together, layer a prepared cream print square over a 2⅞" dark red print square. Sew together ¼" out from each side of the drawn line. Repeat for a total of 510 joined pairs.

Make 510.

3. Cut each pair apart on the drawn line for a total of 1,020 half-square-triangle units. Press the seam allowance toward the red print. Trim away the dog-ear points.

Make 1,020.

4. Lay out four half-square-triangle units, one strip set 1 segment, and two strip set 2 segments in three horizontal rows to form a Churn Dash block. Join the pieces in rows one and three. Press the seam allowances toward the strip-set segments. Join the rows and press the seam allowances toward the center row. Repeat for a total of 255 blocks measuring 5½" square.

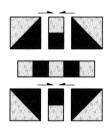

Make 255.

5. Using a mechanical pencil, lightly draw a diagonal line on the wrong side of each 1½" medium red print square.

6. With right sides together, layer a prepared medium red print square over each corner of a Churn Dash block, with raw edges aligned, and stitch together exactly on the drawn lines. Press and trim as instructed in "Pressing Triangle

Units" on page 13. Repeat for a total of 143 embellished blocks.

Embellished Block
Make 143.

7. With right sides together, layer a prepared medium red print square over two adjacent corners of a Churn Dash block. Sew, press, and trim as instructed in step 6. Repeat for a total of 48 half-embellished blocks.

Half-Embellished Block
Make 48.

8. With right sides together, layer a prepared medium red print square over one corner of a Churn Dash block; sew, press, and trim as instructed in step 6. Repeat for a total of four quarter-embellished blocks.

Quarter-Embellished Block
Make 4.

PIECE THE SASHING STRIPS

1. Join a 1" x 39" cream print strip to each opposite end of a 1" x 5½" cream print rectangle. Press the seam allowances away from the center rectangle. Repeat for a total of two cream print sashing strips measuring 1" x 82½" (below).

39"　　5½"　　39"

Make 2.

2. Lay out eleven strip set 3 segments and twelve 1" cream print squares in alternating positions. Join the pieces. Sew a strip set 5 segment in a mirror-image position to each end of the sashing strip. Press all seam allowances toward the red print. Repeat for a total of 14 pieced sashing strips measuring 1" x 82½".

Piece the Rows

1. Lay out 15 unembellished Churn Dash blocks and fourteen 1" x 5½" cream print rectangles in alternating positions. Sew together. Press the seam allowances toward the cream print rectangles. Repeat to form an additional row. Label these row 1 and row 17.

2. Lay out 11 half-embellished Churn Dash blocks and 12 strip set 4 segments in alternating positions. Sew together. Press the seam allowances toward the strip-set segments. Add a quarter-embellished block in a mirror-image position to each end, followed by a 1" x 5½" cream print rectangle and an unembellished Churn Dash block; press the seam allowances away from the blocks. Repeat to form an additional row. Label these row 2 and row 16.

3. Lay out 11 embellished Churn Dash blocks and 12 strip set 3 segments in alternating positions. Sew together. Press the seam allowances toward the strip segments. Add a half-embellished block in a mirror-image position to each end, followed by a 1" x 5½" cream print rectangle and an unembellished Churn Dash block. Press the seam allowances away from the blocks. Repeat to form a total of 13 rows, numbered 3 through 15.

Sashing Strips

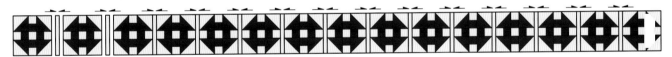

Strip set 5   Strip set 3

Make 14.

Rows 1 and 17

Make 2.

Rows 2 and 16

Unembellished block

Half-embellished block

Quarter-embellished block

Make 2.

Rows 3–15

Unembellished block

Embellished block

Half-embellished block

Make 13.

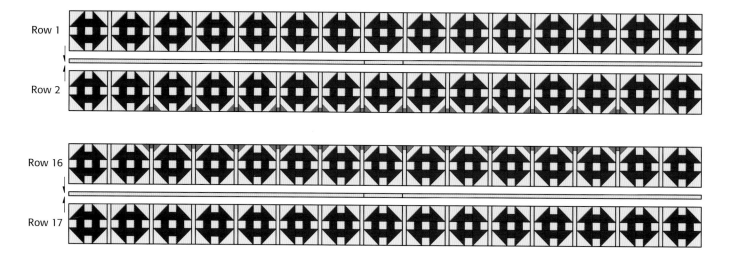

Row 1

Row 2

Row 16

Row 17

Assemble the Quilt Top

1. Lay out row 1 and row 2 and join to each long side of a cream print sashing strip to form a unit. Press the seam allowances toward the sashing strip. Repeat with row 16, row 17, and a second cream print sashing strip (above).

2. Lay out rows 3 through 15 in alternating positions with the 14 pieced sashing strips; join the rows and strips. Press the seam allowances toward the pieced sashing strips.

3. Join the row 1 and row 2 unit to the top of the quilt center. Press the seam allowances toward the sashing strip. Join the row 16 and row 17 unit to the bottom of the quilt center, placing it in a mirror-image position to the rows 1 and 2 unit; press the seam allowance toward the sashing strip. The pieced quilt top should now measure 82½" x 93½".

For a coordinated look, piece some extra Churn Dash blocks and use them to make pillowcases.

COMPLETE THE QUILT

Refer to "Finishing Techniques" on pages 16–20 for details as needed. Layer the quilt top, batting, and backing. Quilt the layers together. Each row of the pictured quilt was machine quilted in a feathered cable pattern, with the direction of each cable alternating row by row. The remaining areas of the quilt top were filled in with an overall meandering stipple pattern. Use the ten 2½" x 42" dark red print strips to bind the quilt.

EVERY HEART BEATS TRUE

Filled with patriotic spirit, this inviting quilt features time-honored and universally loved motifs that bring to mind days gone by.

Finished Quilt Size: 70½" x 70½"

MATERIALS FOR LAP QUILT

Yardages are based on 42"-wide fabric.
- 2¼ yards of dark tan print for House blocks, Flag blocks, Star blocks, and checkerboard
- 1⅞ yards *total* of assorted prints and homespun scraps for blocks, appliqués, and binding
- 1½ yards of light tan print for Flag block, Tree blocks, and checkerboard
- ¾ yard *total* of assorted red print scraps for Flag blocks
- ⅝ yard of dark brown print for inner border
- ½ yard of light green print for Tree blocks
- ½ yard of dark green print for Tree blocks
- 2 fat quarters of green print for appliqués
- 1 fat quarter of dark blue print (or equivalent scraps) for Flag blocks
- ⅛ yard of black print for House blocks
- Assorted brown print scraps for Tree blocks
- Assorted gold print scraps for House blocks
- 4½ yards of fabric for backing
- 76" x 76" square of batting
- ⅜" bias bar

CUTTING

As you cut the pieces listed below, cut an extra 3" square from various prints and homespuns for a total of 60 squares. These will be reserved for the leaf appliqués in the outer border.

To simplify the process, cutting instructions are provided separately for each type of block and area of the quilt. Also note that all strips are cut across the width of the fabric unless otherwise indicated. Refer to page 69 for the appliqué pattern piece.

Star Blocks for the Quilt Center (Make 5)

From the assorted prints and homespuns, cut:
- 40 squares, 3" x 3"
- 5 squares, 5½" x 5½"

From the dark tan print, cut:
- 5 strips, 3" x 42"; crosscut into 20 rectangles, 3" x 5½", and 20 squares, 3" x 3"

House Blocks (Make 5)

From the dark tan print, cut:
- 2 strips, 4½" x 42"; crosscut into 10 squares, 4½" x 4½"

From the assorted prints and homespuns, cut:
- 5 rectangles for roofs, 4½" x 10½"

From *each* of 5 assorted prints and homespuns, cut:
- 1 rectangle for house, 2½" x 10½"
- 3 rectangles for house, 2½" x 4½"
- 1 square for house, 2½" x 2½"

From the black print, cut:
- 2 strips, 2½" x 42"; crosscut into 5 rectangles for doors, 2½" x 4½", and 2 squares for windows, 2½" x 2½"

From the assorted gold print scraps, cut:
- 3 squares for windows, 2½" x 2½"

Flag Blocks (Make 8)

From the light tan print, cut:
- 2 strips, 2½" x 42"; crosscut into 8 rectangles, 2½" x 6½"

From the assorted red print scraps, cut:
- 8 rectangles, 2½" x 6½"
- 16 rectangles, 2½" x 10½"

From the dark blue print, cut:
- 8 squares, 4½" x 4½"

From the dark tan print, cut:
- 3 strips, 2½" x 42"; crosscut into 8 rectangles, 2½" x 10½"

Tree Blocks (Make 7)

From the ½ yard of dark green print, cut:
- 5 strips, 2½" x 42"

From the ½ yard of light green print, cut:
- 5 strips, 2½" x 42"

From the light tan print, cut:
- 4 strips, 2½" x 42"; crosscut into 28 squares, 2½" x 2½", and 14 rectangles, 2½" x 4½"

From the assorted brown print scraps, cut:
- 7 squares, 2½" x 2½"

Inner Border

From the dark brown print, cut:
- 6 strips, 2½" x 42"
- 2 strips, 1½" x 42"; crosscut into 8 rectangles, 1½" x 8½"

Star Blocks for the Border (Make 4)

From the assorted prints and homespuns, cut:
- 32 squares, 2½" x 2½"
- 4 squares, 4½" x 4½"

From the dark tan print, cut:
- 3 strips, 2½" x 42"; crosscut into 16 rectangles, 2½" x 4½", and 16 squares, 2½" x 2½"

Checkerboard Border

From the light tan print, cut:
- 7 strips, 4½" x 42"

From the dark tan print, cut:
- 7 strips, 4½" x 42"

From the reserved 3" assorted print and homespun squares, cut:
- 60 pattern A pieces

Binding

Cut enough 2½"-wide random lengths of assorted prints and homespuns to form a 300" length of binding when joined end to end.

PIECE THE STAR BLOCKS FOR THE QUILT CENTER

1. Using a mechanical pencil, lightly draw a diagonal line on the wrong side of the forty 3" assorted print squares.

2. With right sides together, layer a prepared 3" square over one end of a 3" x 5½" dark tan print rectangle. Sew exactly on the drawn line. Press and trim, referring to "Pressing Triangle Units" on page 13. Repeat for 20 pieced rectangles.

3. Layer a prepared assorted print 3" square on the opposite end of a pieced rectangle to form a mirror-image star point unit. Sew, press, and trim as instructed in step 2. Repeat for a total of 20 star point units.

Make 20.

Every Heart Beats True Lap Quilt

Finished Quilt Size: 70½" x 70½" • Finished Block Size: 10"

Designed, pieced, and machine appliquéd by Kim Diehl. Machine quilted by Kathy Ockerman.

4. Sew a star point unit to opposite sides of an assorted print 5½" square. Press the seam allowances toward the assorted print. Repeat for a total of five star center units.

5. Sew a 3" tan print square to each short end of the remaining star point units. Press the seam allowances toward the tan print squares.

6. Join a unit formed in step 5 to the remaining opposite sides of a star center unit. Press the seam allowances toward the star center. Repeat for a total of five Star blocks measuring 10½" square.

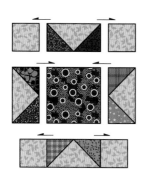 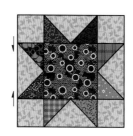

Make 5.

PIECE THE HOUSE BLOCKS

1. Using a mechanical pencil, lightly draw a diagonal line on the wrong side of the ten 4½" dark tan print squares.

2. With right sides together, align a prepared square with each opposite end of a 4½" x 10½" roof rectangle, in mirror-image positions. Sew together exactly on the drawn lines. Press and trim, referring to "Pressing Triangle Units" on page 13. Repeat for a total of five roof units.

 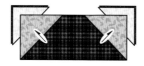

Make 5.

3. Join a 2½" x 4½" house rectangle to each side of a 2½" x 4½" black print rectangle. Press the seam allowance toward the black print. Repeat for a total of five door units.

Make 5.

4. Join a 2½" house square to a 2½" black or gold print square. Press the seam allowance toward the house square. Repeat for a total of five window units.

Make 5.

5. Join a 2½" x 4½" house rectangle to the right long side of each window unit from step 4. Press the seam allowances toward the house rectangle. Repeat for a total of five pieced window units.

Make 5.

6. Join a pieced window unit, with the window positioned at the top, to a door unit from step 3. Press the seam allowance toward the door unit. Repeat for a total of five pieced door-and-window units.

7. Join a 2½" x 10½" house rectangle to the top edge of a door-and-window unit. Press the seam allowance toward the house rectangle. Repeat for a total of five house units.

8. Join a house unit to a roof unit from step 2. Press the seam allowance toward the house unit. Repeat for a total of five House blocks measuring 10½" square.

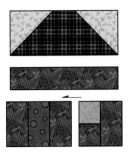 

Make 5.

Piece the Flag Blocks

1. Join a 2½" x 6½" light tan print rectangle to a 2½" x 6½" red print rectangle, sewing together along the long edges. Press the seam allowance toward the red print. Repeat for a total of eight short striped units.

2. Sew a short striped unit to one end of a 4½" dark blue print square. Press the seam allowance toward the blue print. Repeat for a total of eight pieced flag units.

3. Join a 2½" x 10½" red print rectangle to each long edge of a 2½" x 10½" dark tan print rectangle. Press the seam allowances toward the red print. Repeat for a total of eight striped units.

4. Join a pieced flag unit to a striped unit to complete a block. Press the seam allowance toward the red print. Repeat for a total of eight Flag blocks, each measuring 10½" square.

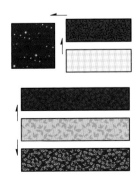 

Make 8.

Piece the Tree Blocks

1. Join three 2½" x 42" dark green print strips and two 2½" x 42" light green print strips to form strip set 1. Press the seam allowances toward the dark green print. Cut the set into fourteen 2½"-wide segments.

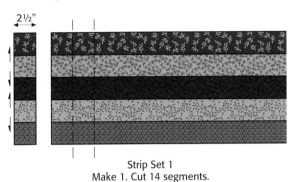

2½"

Strip Set 1
Make 1. Cut 14 segments.

2. Join three 2½" x 42" light green print strips with two 2½" x 42" dark green print strips to form strip set 2. Press the seam allowances toward the dark green print. Cut the set into fourteen 2½"-wide segments.

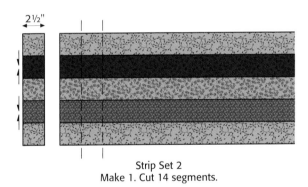

2½"

Strip Set 2
Make 1. Cut 14 segments.

3. Lay out the strip-set segments in the following order: strip set 1, strip set 2, strip set 1, strip set 2. Sew the rows together. Press the seam allowances in one direction. Repeat for a total of seven checkerboard units.

4. Draw a diagonal line on the wrong side of the twenty-eight 2½" light tan print squares. Align a prepared square with the raw edge of each corner

of the checkerboard units. Sew together exactly along the drawn lines. Press and trim, referring to "Pressing Triangle Units" on page 13. Repeat for a total of seven tree-top units.

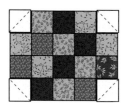 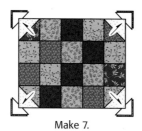

Make 7.

5. Sew a 2½" x 4½" light tan print rectangle to opposite sides of a 2½" brown print square. Press the seam allowances toward the brown print. Repeat for a total of seven trunk units.

6. Join a trunk unit to a tree-top unit to complete the block. Press the seam allowance toward the trunk unit. Repeat for a total of seven Tree blocks measuring 10½" square.

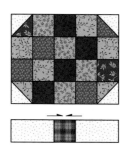 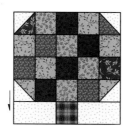

Make 7.

Assemble the Quilt Center

1. Using the quilt photo as a guide, lay out the blocks in five horizontal rows. Join the blocks in each row. Press the seam allowances of each row in alternate directions so that the seams butt together when the rows are joined.

2. Join the rows. Press the seam allowances in one direction. The pieced quilt center should now measure 50½" square.

Add the Inner Border

1. Use the six 2½" x 42" lengths of dark brown print to piece two 50½"-long strips and two 54½"-long strips. Press the seam allowances to one side.

2. Join a 50½"-long strip to the right and left sides of the quilt center. Press the seam allowances toward the brown print.

3. Join a 54½"-long strip to the top and bottom edges of the quilt center. Press the seam allowances toward the brown print. The quilt center with inner borders should now measure 54½" square.

Piece the Checkerboard Border Strips

1. Join a 4½" x 42" light tan strip to a 4½" x 42" dark tan strip to form a strip set. Press the seam allowance toward the dark tan print. Repeat for a total of seven strip sets. Cut the strip sets into fifty-two 4½"-wide segments.

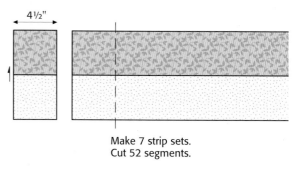

Make 7 strip sets.
Cut 52 segments.

2. Join 13 strip-set segments in alternating positions to form a checkerboard strip. Press the seam allowances in one direction. Repeat for a total of four checkerboard strips.

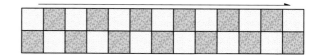

Appliqué the Borders

Referring to "Machine Appliqué Made Easy" on pages 21–24, prepare the appliqués.

1. From the fat quarters of green print, cut enough 1¼"-wide bias lengths to equal four 70" strips when joined end to end. Sew the lengths together. Press the seam allowances open.

2. With wrong sides together, fold each 70"-long strip in half lengthwise and stitch a scant ¼" in from the long raw edges to form a tube. Insert the

bias bar into the tube and slide it along as you press the stem, making sure the seam is centered and lies flat.

3. Using the quilt photo as a guide, use a fabric glue stick to anchor the vines to the four checkerboard units. Appliqué in place, referring to "Invisible Machine Appliqué" on pages 24–26.

4. Position the leaves along the vines and appliqué them to the checkerboard background. Reserve the leaves that overlap onto the inner border for later use.

Piece the Star Blocks for the Border

For *each* of the Star blocks, you will need the following:
- 8 squares, 2½" x 2½", from assorted prints
- 4 dark tan print rectangles, 2½" x 4½"
- 4 dark tan print squares, 2½" x 2½"
- 1 square, 4½" x 4½", from assorted prints

Referring to the illustrations and instructions provided for the quilt center Star blocks on pages 64 and 66, piece four Star blocks for the border corners. These finished blocks should measure 8½" square.

Add the Checkerboard Borders

1. Join a 1½" x 8½" dark brown print rectangle to opposite short ends of each appliquéd checkerboard strip. Press the seam allowances toward the brown print. Join these strips to the right and left sides of the quilt center. Press the seam allowances toward the inner border.

2. Join an 8½" Star block to the brown print at each end of the remaining two checkerboard strips. Press the seam allowances toward the brown print. Join these strips to the top and bottom edges of the quilt center. Press the seam allowances toward the inner border. Appliqué the remaining leaves to the quilt top. The pieced quilt top should now measure 70½" square.

Complete the Quilt

Refer to "Finishing Techniques" on pages 16–20 for details as needed. Layer the quilt top, batting, and backing. Quilt the layers together. The featured quilt was machine quilted in an overall pattern of spiraling circles that resemble cinnamon-roll swirls. Use the 300"-long assorted print strip to bind the quilt.

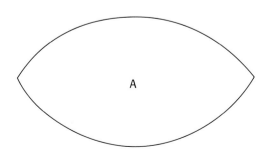

Appliqué Pattern

BUTTONS AND BOWS

Dig deep into your scrap basket

when preparing strips for these little

Log Cabin blocks–the more the merrier!

Notice how the deep, rich colors and

just a sprinkling of light prints

make this quilt come alive.

Finished Quilt Size: 63½" x 63½"

MATERIALS FOR LAP QUILT

Yardages are based on 42"-wide fabric.
- 3¼ yards of assorted prints for blocks
- 1⅞ yards of red print for blocks and border
- 1 yard of tan print for blocks and border
- 4 yards of fabric for backing
- 69" x 69" square of batting
- 49 assorted buttons, if desired

CUTTING

All strips are cut across the width of the fabric unless otherwise noted.

From the assorted prints, cut:
- 49 squares, 1½" x 1½"
- 98 rectangles, 1½" x 2½"
- 98 rectangles, 1½" x 3½"
- 98 rectangles, 1½" x 4½"
- 98 rectangles, 1½" x 5½"
- 98 rectangles, 1½" x 6½"
- 49 rectangles, 1½" x 7½"
- Random lengths of 2½"-wide assorted prints to form 270" length of binding when joined end to end

From the red print, cut:
- 4 strips, 1½" x 42"; crosscut into 49 squares, 1½" x 1½"
- 7 strips, 7½" x 42"; crosscut into 32 squares, 7½" x 7½"

From the tan print, cut:
- 8 strips, 2½" x 42"; crosscut into 128 squares, 2½" x 2½"
- 5 strips, 1½" x 42"; crosscut into 128 squares, 1½" x 1½"

PIECE THE BLOCKS

1. With right sides together, join a 1½" assorted print square to a 1½" red print square. Press the seam allowance toward the assorted print.

Pin Point

To save time as you press, position your ironing board next to your sewing machine at table height. You'll eliminate extra steps!

2. Hold the unit from step 1 with the red print square positioned at the bottom. With right sides together, sew a 1½" x 2½" rectangle to the left side of the unit. Press the seam allowance toward the rectangle, away from the red print square.

3. Working in a counter-clockwise direction, continue adding rectangles around the perimeter of the block, increasing the length of the rectangles to fit the growing size of the block. Press the seam allowances toward each new rectangle, away from the red center.

Pin Point

When adding rectangles 3" in length or more to a Log Cabin block, the side of the block with two seams will always be the side where you join the next piece!

4. Repeat steps 1 through 3 for a total of 49 Log Cabin blocks measuring 7½" square.

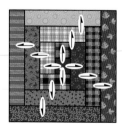

Make 49.

ADD THE BOW TIE CORNERS

For spontaneous and random placement of your blocks, proceed directly to step 1. If you prefer not to be surprised, lay out and arrange your blocks before proceeding. Mark the position of each block as instructed in "Quilt-Top Assembly" on page 14, and keep in mind that odd-numbered blocks will receive the large tan print corners, while the even-numbered blocks will receive the small tan print corners.

1. Using a mechanical pencil, lightly draw a diagonal line on the wrong side of each of the 1½" and 2½" tan print squares.

2. Select 25 of the Log Cabin blocks; layer a prepared 2½" tan print square over the corners of each. Sew together exactly on the drawn lines. Press and trim each block, referring to "Pressing Triangle Units" on page 13.

3. Repeat step 2 with the remaining 24 blocks, using the 1½" prepared tan print squares.

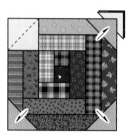 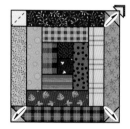

Make 25 with 2½" corners.   Make 24 with 1½" corners.

ASSEMBLE THE QUILT CENTER

Using the quilt photo as a guide, lay out the 49 blocks formed in steps 2 and 3 in alternating positions to make seven rows of seven blocks. Join the blocks in each row; press the seam allowances toward the blocks embellished with the large triangles. Join the rows and press the seam allowances toward the rows that begin and end with the large triangle blocks. The pieced quilt center should now measure 49½" square.

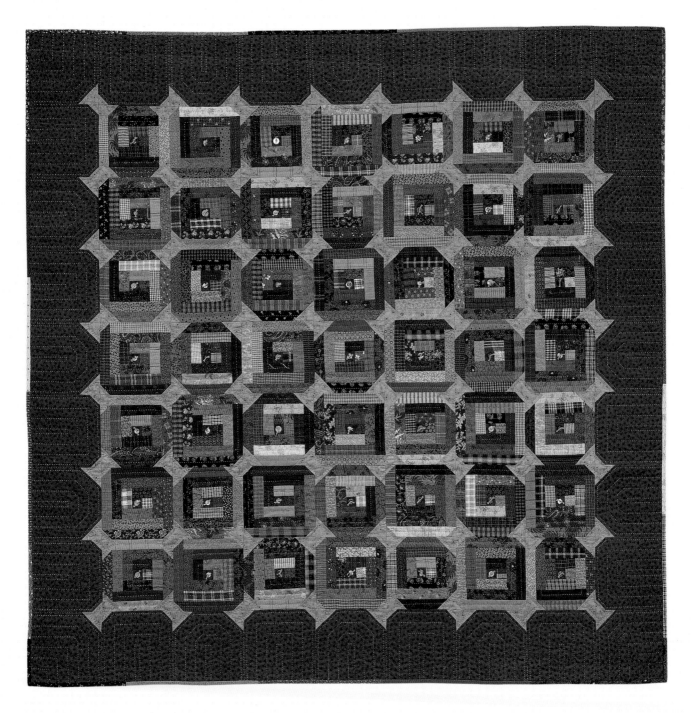

Buttons and Bows Lap Quilt

Finished Quilt Size: 63½" x 63½" • Finished Block Size: 7"

Designed by Kim Diehl. Pieced and hand quilted in the big stitch method by Delene Kohler.

Piece and Add the Borders

1. With right sides together, layer a prepared 2½" tan print square over two adjacent corners of a 7½" red print square. Sew together exactly on the drawn line. Press and trim, referring to "Pressing Triangle Units" on page 13. Repeat for a total of 12 squares embellished with large triangles.

Make 12.

2. Repeat step 1, using the prepared 1½" tan print squares, for a total of 16 squares embellished with small triangles.

Make 16.

3. With right sides together, layer a prepared 2½" tan print square over one corner of a 7½" red print square. Sew, press, and trim as instructed in step 1. Repeat for a total of four corner squares.

Make 4.

4. Lay out four squares with small triangles and three squares with large triangles in alternating positions to form a strip; join the squares. Press the seam allowances toward the blocks with the large triangles. Repeat for a total of four pieced strips.

Make 4.

5. Join a strip to the right and left sides of the quilt center. Press the seam allowances toward the border.

6. Join a corner square to each end of the remaining border strips, with the triangle positioned to the inside. Press the seam allowances toward the corner squares. Sew these strips to the top and bottom of the quilt center. Press the seam allowances toward the border. The finished quilt top should now measure 63½" square.

COMPLETE THE QUILT

Refer to "Finishing Techniques" on pages 16–20 for details as needed. Layer the quilt top, batting, and backing. Quilt the layers together. The featured quilt was hand quilted using perle cotton and the big-stitch method, with concentric squares placed over the center of each Log Cabin row. The border was echo quilted in a horseshoe shape, with the lines radiating out from the sewn seams.

If desired, stitch a button to the red center square of each block, using a double strand of cotton thread or one strand of perle cotton. Tie the ends into a square knot and leave the thread tails visible for a homemade or old-fashioned look.

Use the 270" length of pieced binding to bind the quilt.

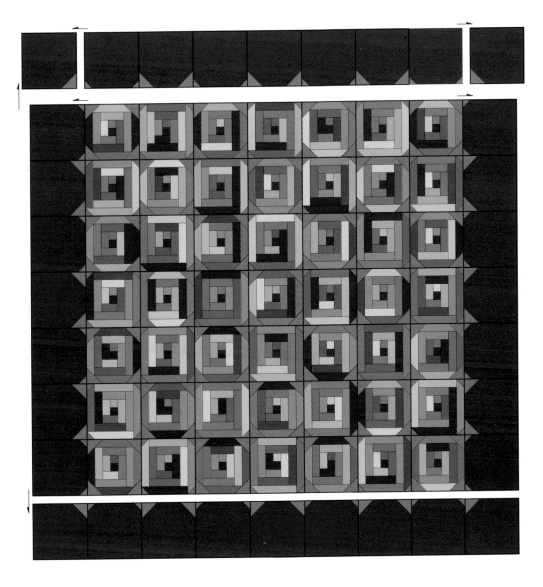

BRICKS AND STONES

This easily pieced quilt uses just two blocks but provides a wonderful array of secondary patterns. Can you find the hidden stars sparkling among the plaids and calicoes?

Finished Quilt Size: 68½" x 68½"

MATERIALS FOR LAP QUILT

Yardages are based on 42"-wide fabric.
- 4½ yards *total* of assorted medium and dark prints for blocks, border, and binding
- 3¾ yards *total* of assorted light prints for blocks and border
- 4¼ yards of fabric for backing
- 74" x 74" square of batting

CUTTING

All strips are cut across the width of the fabric unless otherwise noted.

From the assorted medium and dark prints, cut:
- 206 squares, 2½" x 2½"
- 26 squares, 5¼" x 5¼"; cut each square in half diagonally to yield 52 half-square triangles
- 48 rectangles, 2½" x 4½"
- 48 rectangles, 4½" x 8½"
- 16 squares, 3⅜" x 3⅜"
- Random lengths of assorted 2½"-wide medium and dark prints to equal 290" of binding when pieced end to end

From the assorted light prints, cut:
- 26 squares, 4" x 4"; cut each square in half diagonally to yield 52 half-square triangles
- 48 rectangles, 2½" x 4½"
- 154 squares, 2½" x 2½"
- 96 squares, 4½" x 4½"
- 8 squares, 5¼" x 5¼"; cut each square in half diagonally to yield 16 half-square triangles

PIECE THE SQUARE-IN-A-SQUARE BLOCKS

1. With right sides together, join two 2½" medium and dark print squares. Press the seam allowance to one side. Repeat for a total of 26 two-patch units.

2. With right sides together, layer together two of the two-patch units with the center seams butting together and join. Press the seam allowance to one side. Repeat for a total of 13 four-patch units.

3. Gently fold the long side of an assorted light print 4" triangle in half to find the center, and finger-press a crease. Align this crease with the center seam at one edge of a four-patch unit; pin in place and stitch together. Press the seam allowance toward the triangle. Repeat with the opposite side of the four-patch unit. Then add 4" triangles to opposite sides to form a square-in-a-square unit. Repeat for a total of 13 units.

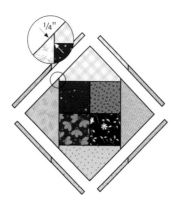

4. Use a rotary cutter and acrylic ruler to trim the seam allowance at the point of each side of the square-in-a-square units to ¼", taking care that the units remain square.

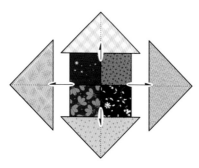

5. Join an assorted medium or dark print 5¼" triangle to each side of a square-in-a-square unit as instructed in steps 3 and 4. Repeat for a total of 13 Square-in-a-Square blocks measuring 8½" square.

Make 13.

PIECE THE RAIL FENCE BLOCKS

1. Join a 2½" x 4½" light and dark print rectangle together along one long edge. Press the seam allowance toward the dark print. Repeat for a total of 48 pairs.

2. Lay out four rectangle pairs to form a Rail Fence block, with the light and dark prints positioned randomly. Join the pairs in each row. Press the seam allowances of the top and bottom rows toward the whole rectangles. Join the rows and press the center seam open. Repeat for a total of 12 Rail Fence blocks measuring 8½" square.

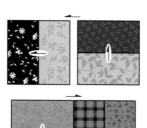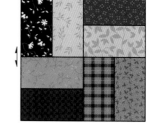

Make 12.

PIECE THE CHECKERBOARD SEGMENTS AND SASHING STRIPS

1. Join two 2½" light and two 2½" dark print squares in alternating positions to form a checkerboard segment. Press the seam allowances toward the dark print. Repeat for a total of 34 segments.

Make 34.

Bricks and Stones Lap Quilt

Finished Quilt Size: 68½" x 68½" • Finished Block Size: 8"

Designed by Kim Diehl and pieced by Darlene Bott. Machine quilted by Kathy Ockerman.

2. Join thirteen 2½" light and thirteen 2½" dark print squares in alternating positions to form a checkerboard sashing strip. Press the seam allowances toward the dark print. Repeat for a total of four sashing strips measuring 52½" long.

3. Join seventeen 2½" light and seventeen 2½" dark print squares as instructed in step 2. Repeat for a total of two sashing strips measuring 68½" long.

ASSEMBLE THE QUILT CENTER

1. Lay out three Square-in-a-Square blocks, two Rail Fence blocks, and six checkerboard segments to form a row. Join the blocks and segments. Press the seam allowances in one direction. Repeat for a total of three rows.

Make 3 rows.

Pin Point

When the size of a block or a pieced unit is inaccurate, make several small seam adjustments instead of one large correction. This will keep your grid proportions intact.

2. Lay out three Rail Fence blocks, two Square-in-a-Square blocks, and six checkerboard segments to form a row. Join the blocks and segments. Press the seam allowances in one direction. Repeat for a total of two rows.

Make 2 rows.

3. Lay out the rows in alternating positions. Add four 52½" checkerboard sashing strips, placing one between each row. Join the rows and sashing strips. Press the seam allowances toward the checkerboard sashing strips. The pieced quilt center should now measure 52½" square.

PIECE THE BORDERS

To piece the flying-geese units and flying-geese strips, follow these steps:

1. Use a mechanical pencil to lightly draw a diagonal line on the wrong side of each of the assorted 96 light print 4½" squares.

2. With right sides together, lay a prepared 4½" square over one end of an assorted dark print 4½" x 8½" rectangle. Sew together exactly on the drawn line. Press and trim, referring to "Pressing Triangle Units" on page 13. With right sides together, lay a prepared 4½" square over the opposite end of the dark print rectangle in a mirror-image position. Sew, press, and trim as before. Repeat for a total of 96 flying-geese units.

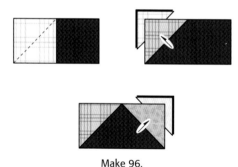

Make 96.

3. Lay out 12 flying-geese units, with six of the units in a mirror-image position. Join the units to form a strip. Press the seam allowances away from the points toward the dark print, and press the center seam open. Repeat for a total of four flying-geese strips.

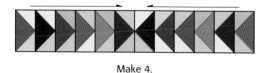

Make 4.

To piece the Square-in-a-Square border blocks, follow these steps:

1. Use four assorted medium and dark print 3⅜" squares to form a four-patch unit as in steps 1 and 2 of "Piece the Square-in-a-Square Blocks" on page 77. Repeat for a total of four of the four-patch units.

2. Join an assorted light print 5¼" triangle to each side of the four-patch unit and trim the seam allowances as instructed in step 3 of "Piece the Square-in-a-Square Blocks" on page 78. Repeat for a total of four blocks measuring 8½" square.

COMPLETE THE QUILT TOP

1. Join a flying-geese strip to the right and left sides of the quilt center. Press the seam allowances toward the checkerboard sashing strips.

2. Lay out a flying-geese strip, two checkerboard segments, and two Square-in-a-Square border blocks to form a strip. Join the pieces. Press the seam allowances toward the checkerboard segments.

Make 2.

3. Join a 68½" checkerboard sashing strip to the top and bottom of the quilt center. Press the seam allowances toward the sashing strips. Join a strip from step 2 to the top and bottom of the quilt. Press the seam allowances toward the checkerboard sashing strips. The finished quilt top should now measure 68½" square.

COMPLETE THE QUILT

Refer to "Finishing Techniques" on pages 16–20 for details as needed. Layer the quilt top, batting, and backing. Quilt the layers together. The featured quilt was machine quilted in a meandering stipple pattern with randomly placed motifs, such as flowers, feathered plumes, and stars. Use the 290" length of pieced binding to bind the quilt.

Five-Cent Fairy Garden

Even the tiniest scraps from your favorite homespuns, ticking stripes, and plaids can be included in this cheery little quilt. And remember your nickel for perfectly shaped berries and flower centers!

Finished Candle Mat Size: 21½" x 21½"

Materials for Candle Mat

Yardages are based on 42"-wide fabric.
- ½ yard of medium or dark homespun for inner border and binding
- 40 assorted homespun squares, 1½" x 1½", for the quilt center
- 30 assorted homespun rectangles, 1½" x 2½", for the quilt center
- 4 assorted tan homespun rectangles, 5½" x 11½", for the outer border
- 4 assorted tan homespun squares, 5½" x 5½", for the outer border
- Assorted homespun scraps for appliqué
- Assorted green homespun scraps for appliqué
- ¾ yard of fabric for backing
- 27" x 27" piece of batting
- One nickel (appliqué template)
- ⅜" bias bar

Cutting

All strips are cut across the width of the fabric unless otherwise noted. Refer to page 87 for the appliqué pattern pieces.

From the ½ yard of medium or dark homespun, cut:
- 2 strips, 1" x 10½"
- 2 strips, 1" x 11½"
- 6 strips, 2½" x 18"

From the assorted homespun scraps, cut:
- 4 pattern A pieces
- 4 pattern D pieces
- 4 pattern E pieces
- 4 pattern G pieces
- 4 pattern H pieces
- 24 circles traced with a nickel

From the assorted green homespun scraps, cut:
- 16 pattern B pieces
- 8 pattern C pieces
- 4 pattern F pieces
- 8 bias strips, 1½" x 10"

PIECE THE CANDLE MAT CENTER

Lay out forty 1½" assorted homespun squares and thirty 1½" x 2½" assorted homespun rectangles to form four rows of squares and three rows of rectangles, with 10 pieces in each row. Join the pieces in each row. Press the seam allowances of each row in alternating directions. Join the rows and press the seam allowances in one direction. The pieced candle mat center should measure 10½" square.

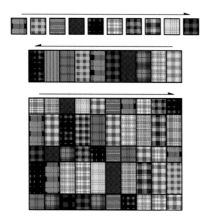

ADD THE BORDERS

1. Join a 1" x 10½" medium or dark homespun strip to the right and left sides of the candle mat center. Press the seam allowances toward the strips. Join a 1" x 11½" strip to the top and bottom of the candle mat center. Press the seam allowances toward the strips.

2. Join a 5½" x 11½" assorted tan homespun rectangle to the right and left sides of the quilt top. Press the seam allowances toward the dark strips.

3. Join a 5½" x 5½" assorted tan homespun square to each short end of the two remaining tan homespun rectangles to form a strip. Press the seam allowances toward the squares.

4. Join the pieced border strips to the top and bottom of the quilt top. Press the seam allowances toward the dark inner-border strips.

APPLIQUÉ THE BORDERS

Referring to "Machine Appliqué Made Easy" on pages 21–24, prepare the appliqués.

1. With *wrong* sides together, fold each 1½" x 10" green homespun strip in half lengthwise and stitch a scant ¼" in from the long raw edges to form a tube. Insert the bias bar into the tube and slide it along as you press the stem, making sure the seam is centered and lies flat. Fold under the raw edge at one end about ¼" and use a fabric glue stick to anchor it in place.

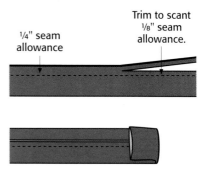

¼" seam allowance

Trim to scant ⅛" seam allowance.

Pin Point

Whenever a pattern instructs you to sew a fabric tube for use with a bias bar, use a scant ¼" seam allowance. This will allow the bar to move easily through the tube and may eliminate the need to trim the seam allowance.

2. Using the quilt photo as a guide and referring to "Invisible Machine Appliqué" on pages 24–26, lay out the appliqués and prepared stems. Begin stitching with the appliqués cut with pattern C. Then proceed to the 10" stems. As the remaining appliqués are stitched in place, they will cover the unfinished ends of the stems positioned in the corners.

Five-Cent Fairy Garden Candle Mat

Finished Candle Mat Size: 21½" x 21½"

Designed, pieced, machine appliquéd, and hand quilted by Kim Diehl.

Complete the Candle Mat

Refer to "Finishing Techniques" on pages 16–20 for details as needed. Layer the quilt top, batting, and backing. Quilt the layers together. The featured quilt was hand quilted with diagonal lines through the center squares and rectangles to form kite shapes. The borders were echo quilted to emphasize the appliqués. Use the six 2½" x 18" strips to bind the quilt.

Appliqué Patterns

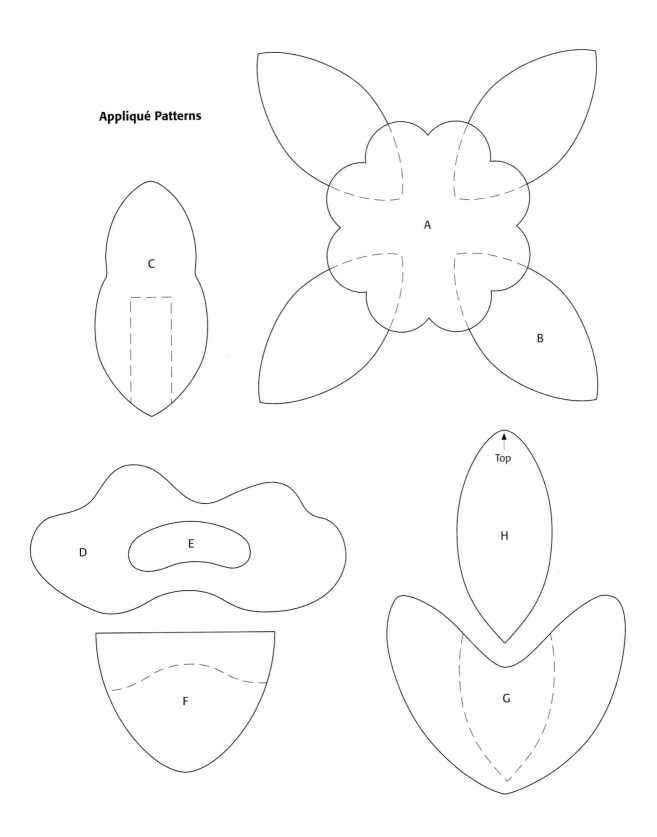

COLONIAL COCKSCOMB

Soft, tomato-red blooms and gentle pea-green stems evoke memories of quilting bees, tatted lace, and your grandmother's best quilts airing in the summer sunshine. Add coordinating pillowcases and a matching throw pillow for a beautifully traditional look.

Finished Quilt Size: 88½" x 94½"

MATERIALS FOR BED QUILT

Yardages are based on 42"-wide fabric.
- 8½ yards of cream print for background
- 4 yards of dark red print for patchwork, appliqués, and binding
- 4¼ yards of green print for appliqués
- 1⅝ yards of medium red print for appliqués
- ⅞ yard of light red print for appliqués
- 8 yards of fabric for backing (3 widths pieced horizontally)
- 94" x 100" piece of batting

Pin Point

Are you having trouble finding fabric in just the right color for your quilt? The wrong side of a printed fabric may provide you with the perfect color option!

CUTTING

All strips are cut across the width of the fabric unless otherwise noted. Refer to pages 94–95 for the appliqué pattern pieces.

From the cream print, cut:
- 20 squares, 16½" x 16½"
- 9 strips, 2½" x 42"; crosscut into 144 squares, 2½" x 2½"
- 2 strips, 10½" x 80½", from the *lengthwise* grain
- 1 strip, 10½" x 64½", from the *lengthwise* grain
- 2 squares, 12½" x 12½"
- 2 rectangles, 2½" x 12½"

From the dark red print, cut:
- 9 strips, 2½" x 42"; crosscut into 72 rectangles, 2½" x 4½"
- 10 strips, 2½" x 42"
- 110 pattern A pieces
- 80 pattern E pieces
- 20 pattern G pieces

From the green print, cut:
- 80 pattern D pieces for blocks
- 30 pattern D pieces for border
- 80 pattern F pieces

From the medium red print, cut:
- 110 pattern B pieces
- 20 pattern H pieces

From the light red print, cut:
- 110 pattern C pieces
- 20 pattern I pieces

Appliqué the Blocks

Referring to "Machine Appliqué Made Easy" on pages 21–24, prepare the appliqués. Using the quilt photo as a guide and referring to "Invisible Machine Appliqué" on pages 24–26, lay out and begin stitching the appliqués to the 16½" cream print squares.

Piece the Quilt Center

1. Join four Colonial Cockscomb blocks to form a row. Press the seam allowances in one direction. Repeat to form a total of five rows.

2. Lay out the rows to form the quilt center, positioning the rows so that the seams lie in alternating directions and butt together. Join the rows. Press the seam allowances in one direction. The pieced quilt center should measure 64½" x 80½".

Piece the Sawtooth Border

1. Using a mechanical pencil, lightly draw a diagonal line on the wrong side of the 144 cream print 2½" squares.

2. With right sides together, layer a prepared 2½" cream print square over one end of a 2½" x 4½" dark red print rectangle. Sew together exactly on the drawn line. Press and trim, referring to "Pressing Triangle Units" on page 13. Repeat for a total of 72 pieced rectangles.

3. Layer a prepared 2½" cream print square on the opposite end of a dark red print rectangle in a mirror-image position. Sew, press, and trim as instructed in step 2. Repeat for a total of 72 sawtooth units.

Make 72.

4. Join 20 sawtooth units end to end to form a strip. Press the seam allowances to one side. Repeat for a total of two sawtooth strips measuring 80½" long.

Make 2.

5. Join 16 sawtooth units as instructed in step 4. Repeat for a total of two Sawtooth strips measuring 64½" long.

Piece and Appliqué the Border Strips

1. Join an 80½" sawtooth strip to a 10½" x 80½" cream print strip, with the points of the red triangles joined to the cream strip. Press the seam allowances toward the cream print. Repeat for a total of two border strips measuring 80½" long.

2. Join and press a 64½" sawtooth strip to a 10½" x 64½" cream print strip as instructed in step 1. Reserve the second 64½" sawtooth strip for later use.

3. Referring to the quilt photo as a guide, lay out and appliqué 28 Colonial Cockscomb flowers to the borders, placing the stems so that their unfinished ends are flush with the raw edges of the sawtooth border.

4. With right sides together, lightly press a diagonal valley crease into the two cream print 12½" squares. Position a flower over the crease of each square, with the stem end flush with the point of the square. Appliqué the flowers in place, leaving the bottom 2" to 3" unstitched. Gently fold the unstitched portion of each stem back from the corner and pin it to the background to secure it away from the seam allowance.

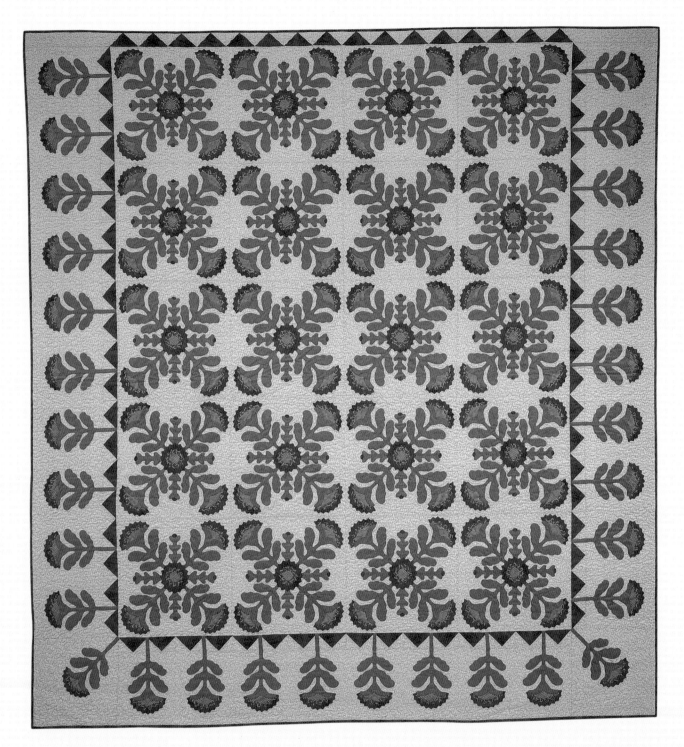

Colonial Cockscomb Bed Quilt

Finished Quilt Size: 88½" x 94½" • Finished Block Size: 16"

Designed, pieced, and machine appliquéd by Kim Diehl. Machine quilted by Kathy Ockerman.

ADD THE BORDERS
TO THE QUILT CENTER

1. Sew the reserved sawtooth strip to the top of the quilt center, aligning the long edges of the red triangles to the blocks. Press the seam allowances toward the quilt center.

2. Sew the long end of a 2½" x 12½" cream print rectangle to one end of an 80½" appliquéd border strip. Press the seam allowance toward the rectangle. Repeat with the second 80½" strip to form a mirror-image border.

Right Border

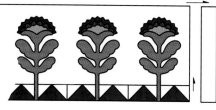

Left Border

3. Join the strips from step 2 to the sides of the quilt center, with the 2½" x 12½" cream print rectangles positioned at the top. Press the seam allowances toward the quilt center.

4. Join a 12½" appliquéd square to each end of the 64½" border strip, with the appliqués in mirror-image positions. Press the seam allowances toward the 12½" squares.

5. Join the strip from step 4 to the bottom of the quilt center. Press the seam allowance toward the quilt center. Unpin the green stems at the border corners and fold under the raw edges to align them with the corners of the sawtooth border. Appliqué in place. The finished quilt top should now measure 88½" x 96½".

COMPLETE THE QUILT

Refer to "Finishing Techniques" on pages 16–20 for details as needed. Layer the quilt top, batting, and backing. Quilt the layers together. The background areas of the featured quilt were machine quilted in an overall meandering stipple pattern to emphasize the appliqués. Use the ten 2½" x 42" strips to bind the quilt.

Pin Points

It's easy to create a coordinating throw pillow. Simply appliqué an extra Colonial Cockscomb block and add sawtooth borders. Quilt the pillow top, add a backing, and lightly stuff with fiberfill.

⟨⟨◦⟩⟩

Complete your bedroom ensemble by piecing sawtooth strips and using them to make pillowcases.

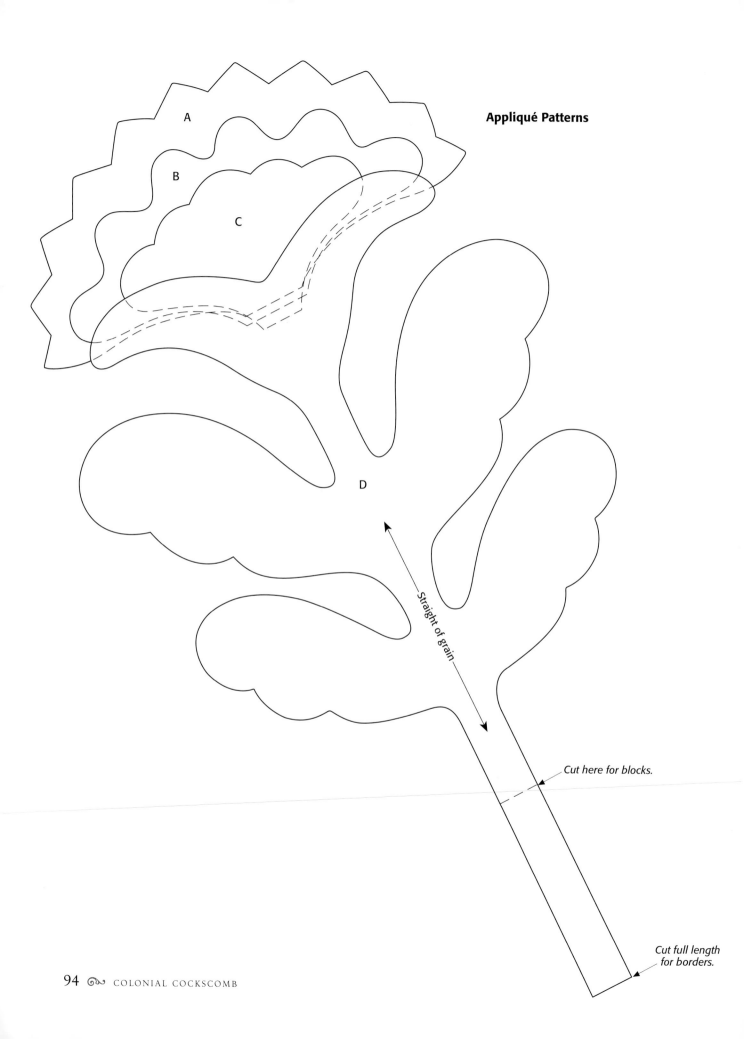

Appliqué Patterns

A

B

C

D

Straight of grain

Cut here for blocks.

Cut full length
for borders.

Appliqué Patterns

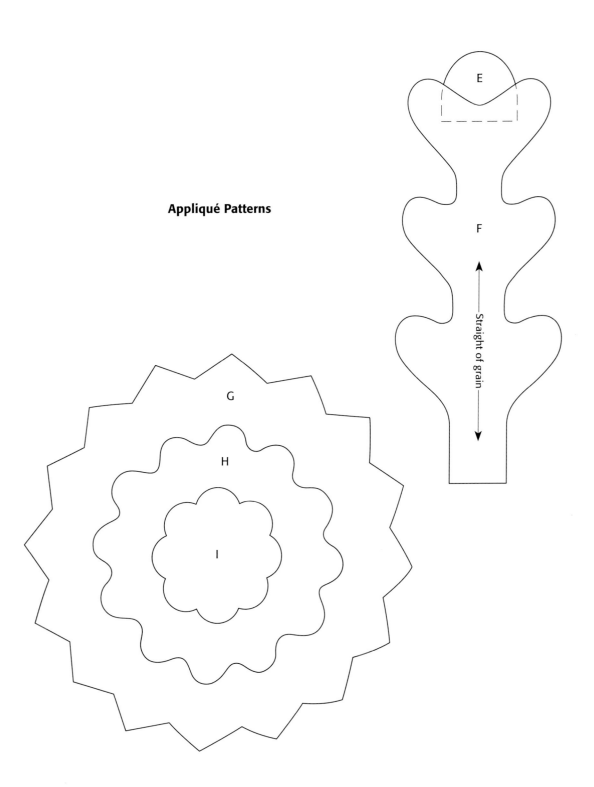

E

F

Straight of grain

G

H

I

COUNTRY WHIG ROSE

This berry-embellished wall hanging frames vibrantly colored appliqués against a sampling of softly muted background prints for a little wall hanging with undeniable charm.

Finished Wall-Hanging Size: 42½" x 42½"

MATERIALS FOR WALL HANGING

Yardages are based on 42"-wide fabric.
- 1⅛ yards of medium green print for outer border and binding
- ⅝ yard of medium-light background print for inner border
- 4 fat quarters of assorted prints for inner border and appliqués
- 4 fat quarters of assorted light prints for block backgrounds
- 4 fat eighths of assorted dark prints for appliqués
- Assorted light print scraps for outer-border corners
- Assorted print scraps for appliqués and inner border
- Assorted green print scraps for appliqués
- 2¾ yards of fabric for backing
- 48" x 48" square of batting
- ⅜" bias bar

CUTTING

All strips are cut across the width of the fabric unless otherwise noted. Refer to page 101 for the appliqué pattern pieces.

Cutting for 1 Whig Rose Block

Repeat with a different set of fabrics for each block. Make 4 blocks total.

From 1 light fat quarter, cut:
- 1 square, 12½" x 12½"

From 1 dark fat eighth, cut:
- 4 pattern A pieces

From the assorted print scraps, cut:
- 4 matching pattern B pieces
- 4 matching pattern C pieces
- 4 matching pattern D pieces
- 4 matching pattern E pieces
- 4 matching pattern F pieces
- 8 matching pattern G pieces
- 8 matching pattern H pieces
- 4 strips, 1¼" x 6", for stems (16 total)

Cutting for Borders

From the medium-light background print, cut:
- 4 strips, 4½" x 42"; crosscut into 12 squares, 4½" x 4½", and 8 rectangles, 4½" x 8½"

From *each* of the 4 assorted print fat quarters, cut:
- 4 squares, 4½" x 4½" (16 total)

From *each* of 4 assorted print scraps, cut:
- 2 squares, 2½" x 2½" (8 total)

From the medium green print, cut:
- 4 strips, 5½" x 42"; trim each to 32½" long
- 5 strips, 2½" x 42"

From *each* of 4 different light print scraps, cut:
- 1 square, 5½" x 5½" (4 total)

From the assorted green print scraps, cut
- 8 strips, 1" x 10"
- 16 pattern G pieces (8 matching pairs)

From the remaining dark prints and assorted print scraps, cut:
- 4 pattern C pieces
- 4 pattern D pieces
- 4 pattern E pieces
- 8 pattern F pieces (4 matching pairs)
- 48 pattern H pieces (8 sets of 6 matching berries)

Appliqué the Blocks

Referring to "Machine Appliqué Made Easy" on pages 21–24, prepare the appliqués.

1. With wrong sides together, fold each 1¼" x 6" print strip in half lengthwise and stitch a scant ¼" in from the long raw edges to form tubes. Trim the seam allowances to ⅛". Insert the bias bar into each tube and slide it along as you press the stem, making sure the seam is centered and lies flat. Repeat using the 1" x 10" green strips.

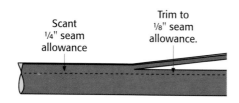

Scant ¼" seam allowance

Trim to ⅛" seam allowance.

Pin Point

When you select an ironing board, choose one with a firm, flat surface rather than a soft, thick pad. This will prevent stretching and distortion of your fabrics as you press.

2. Using the quilt photo as a guide and referring to "Invisible Machine Appliqué" on pages 24–26, lay out and stitch the prepared appliqué pieces to a 12½" light print background square. Repeat for a total of four blocks.

Piece the Wall-Hanging Center

Sew the blocks together in two horizontal rows of two blocks each. Press the seam allowances in alternating directions so that they butt together. Join the rows and press the seam allowance to one side. The pieced wall-hanging center should now measure 24½" square.

Piece and Add the Inner Border

1. Using a mechanical pencil, lightly draw a diagonal line on the wrong side of each 4½" dark print square.

2. With right sides together, layer a prepared 4½" square over one end of a 4½" x 8½" background print rectangle. Sew together exactly on the drawn line. Press and trim, referring to "Pressing Triangle Units" on page 13.

3. Repeat for a total of eight pieced rectangles. Layer a prepared 4½" background print square on the opposite end of the pieced rectangle to form a mirror-image star point. Sew, press, and trim as instructed in step 2. Repeat for a total of eight star point units, two from each assorted print.

Country Whig Rose Wall Hanging

Finished Wall-Hanging Size: 42½" x 42½" • Finished Block Size: 12"

Designed, pieced, machine appliquéd, and hand quilted by Kim Diehl.

4. Using a mechanical pencil, lightly draw a diagonal line on the wrong side of each 2½" assorted print scrap square.

5. With right sides together, layer a prepared square over one corner of a 4½" background print square, aligning the corners. Sew, press, and trim as instructed in step 2. Repeat with a second prepared square and second background square. Repeat for a total of eight pairs, two from each assorted print.

6. Lay out the star point units, step 5 units, and four 4½" background print squares around the quilt center to form the middle border rows. Join the units on the right and left sides to form rows. Press the seam allowances of the star point units toward the background print, and the center triangle seams to one side. Join these rows to the right and left sides of the wall-hanging center. Press the seam allowances toward the quilt center.

7. Sew and press the units to form the top and bottom rows as instructed in step 6. Press the seam allowances of the corner squares toward the background print. Join the rows to the remaining sides of the wall-hanging center and press the seam allowances toward the wall-hanging center. The pieced wall-hanging top should now measure 32½" square.

ADD THE OUTER BORDERS

1. Fold each 5½" x 32½" medium green print strip in half lengthwise with right sides together and use a hot, dry iron to lightly press a valley crease along the center fold.

2. Join a prepared medium green print strip to the right and left sides of the wall-hanging top. Press the seam allowances toward the green strips.

3. Join the 5½" assorted light print squares to each end of the remaining 5½" x 32½" green print strips. Press the seam allowances toward the green print. Join these pieced strips to the remaining sides of the wall-hanging top. Press the seam allowances toward the green print.

COMPLETE THE APPLIQUÉ

Using the project photo as a guide and the pressed creases for centering, work from the bottom layer to the top to appliqué the remaining prepared pattern pieces to the outer border.

COMPLETE THE WALL HANGING

Refer to "Finishing Techniques" on pages 16–20 for details as needed. Layer the wall-hanging top, batting, and backing. Quilt the layers together. The featured wall hanging was hand quilted around the appliqués to emphasize their shape, and concentric squares were placed over the background areas. An adaptation of the appliqué pattern was quilted into the open border areas for a shadow effect. Use the five 2½" x 42" green print strips to bind the wall hanging. If you wish to add a hanging sleeve, please refer to "Making a Hanging Sleeve" on pages 19–20.

Appliqué Patterns

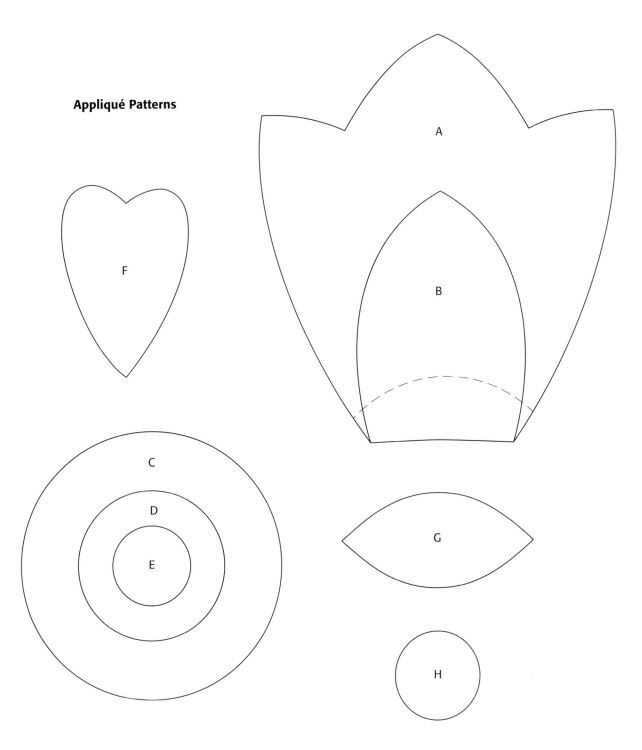

ROMANCE AND ROSES

Capture the romance of a cottage garden when you stitch this lap quilt and coordinating floor pillow (see page 110) ripe with cabbage roses. Choose sun-warmed shades of cranberry, salmon, plum, and gold for lavish blooms that never fade.

Finished Quilt Size: 72½" x 72½"

MATERIALS FOR LAP QUILT

Yardages are based on 42"-wide fabric.
- 6 yards of tan print for blocks and border
- 2¼ yards of light green print for blocks, border, and appliqués
- 2¼ yards of medium green print for blocks, border, appliqués, and binding
- ½ yard *total* of assorted gold prints for blocks and appliqués
- ½ yard *total* of assorted cranberry prints for blocks and appliqués
- ½ yard *total* of assorted plum prints for blocks and appliqués
- ½ yard *total* of assorted salmon prints for blocks and appliqués
- 4⅓ yards of fabric for backing
- 78" x 78" square of batting
- ⅜" bias bar

NOTE: For added interest, a look-alike medium green print was substituted in a handful of blocks and appliqués in the photo quilt.

CUTTING

All strips are cut across the width of the fabric unless otherwise noted. Refer to page 113 for the appliqué pattern pieces.

From *each* assortment of gold, cranberry, plum, and salmon prints, cut:
- 8 squares, 2½" x 2½"
- 64 squares, 1½" x 1½"

From the assorted gold prints, cut:
- 20 pattern A pieces
- 10 pattern B pieces
- 10 pattern C pieces

From the assorted cranberry prints, cut:
- 20 pattern A pieces
- 10 pattern B pieces
- 10 pattern C pieces

From the assorted plum prints, cut:
- 20 pattern A pieces
- 10 pattern B pieces
- 10 pattern C pieces

From the assorted salmon prints, cut:
- 20 pattern A pieces
- 10 pattern B pieces
- 10 pattern C pieces

From the tan print, cut:
- 51 strips, 1½" x 42"; crosscut into 128 rectangles, 1½" x 2½"; 256 rectangles, 1½" x 4½"; and 128 squares, 1½" x 1½". Set aside the remaining 6 strips for later use in the blocks.
- 19 strips, 2½" x 42"; crosscut into 244 squares, 2½" x 2½". Set aside the remaining 3 strips for later use in the blocks.
- 2 strips, 1½" x 48½", from the *length* of the fabric

(Continued) From the tan print, cut:
- 2 strips, 1½" x 50½", from the *length* of the fabric
- 2 strips, 7½" x 54½", from the *length* of the fabric
- 2 strips, 7½" x 68½", from the *length* of the fabric

From the light green print, cut:
- 35 strips, 1½" x 42"; crosscut into 592 squares, 1½" x 1½", and 16 strips, 1½" x 18". Set aside the remaining 4 strips for later use in the blocks.
- 2 strips, 2½" x 42"

From the medium green print, cut:
- 9 strips, 2½" x 42" (reserve 8 for binding)
- 27 strips, 1½" x 42"; crosscut into 640 squares, 1½" x 1½". Set aside the remaining 2 strips for later use in the blocks.
- 80 pattern E pieces

PIECE THE FRAMED NINE PATCH BLOCK

Please note that the assorted prints used within each block are from one color family.

1. Lay out one 2½" assorted print square, four 1½" assorted print squares, and four 1½" x 2½" tan print rectangles to form a nine-patch unit. Join the pieces in each horizontal row. Press the seam allowances toward the dark print. Then join the rows and press the seam allowances toward the center row. Repeat for a total of 8 nine-patch units from each color family resulting in a combined total of 32.

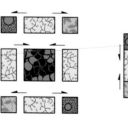

Make 8 from each color family.

2. Join a 1½" x 4½" tan print rectangle to opposite sides of each nine-patch unit. Press the seam allowances toward the tan print.

3. Join a 1½" assorted print square to each end of a 1½" x 4½" tan print rectangle, with both squares from the same color family used in the nine-patch unit. Press the seam allowances toward the tan print. Repeat for a total of 64 pieced rectangle strips.

4. Join a pieced rectangle strip to the remaining sides of a nine-patch unit, keeping the colors consistent within the block. Press the seam allowances toward the rectangle strips. Repeat for a total of 32 Framed Nine Patch blocks measuring 6½" square.

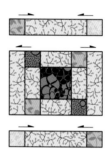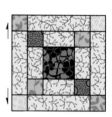

Make 32.

PIECE THE STAR BLOCK

1. Join one 1½" x 42" tan print strip to each side of one 2½" x 42" light green print strip to form a light strip set A. Press the seam allowances toward the light green print. Repeat for a total of two light strip set As.

Light Strip Set A
Make 2.

2. Join two 1½" x 42" light green print strips and one 2½" x 42" tan print strip as instructed in step 1 to form a light strip set B. Press the seam allowances toward the light green print. Repeat for a total of two light strip set Bs.

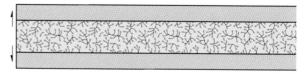

Light Strip Set B
Make 2.

Romance and Roses Lap Quilt

Finished Quilt Size: 72½" x 72½" • Finished Block Size: 6"

Designed by Kim Diehl. Pieced and machine appliquéd by Terry Anderson.
Machine quilted by Kathy Ockerman.

3. Repeat step 1, using two 1½" x 42" tan print strips and one 2½" x 42" medium green print strip to form one medium strip set A. Repeat step 2 using two 1½" x 42" medium green print strips and one 2½" x 42" tan print strip to form a medium strip set B.

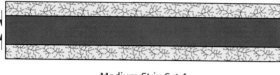

Medium Strip Set A
Make 1.

Medium Strip Set B
Make 1.

4. Cut the light strip set As into 44 segments, 1½" wide. Cut the medium strip set As into 20 segments, 1½" wide.

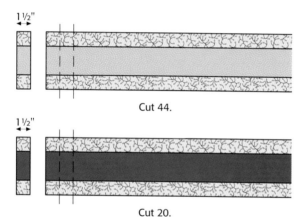

1½"

Cut 44.

1½"

Cut 20.

5. Cut the light strip set Bs into 22 segments, 2½" wide. Cut the medium strip set Bs into 10 segments, 2½" wide.

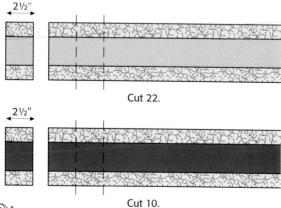

2½"

Cut 22.

2½"

Cut 10.

6. Lay out two strip set A segments and one strip set B segment with the same color value (light or medium) to form a nine-patch unit. Join the rows and press the seam allowances away from the block center. Repeat for a total of 22 light nine-patch units and 10 medium nine-patch units, for a total of 32.

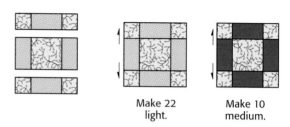

Make 22
light.

Make 10
medium.

7. Using a mechanical pencil, lightly draw a diagonal line on the wrong side of 176 light green print 1½" squares and 80 medium green print 1½" squares.

8. With right sides together, layer a prepared 1½" light green square over each end of a 1½" x 4½" tan print rectangle in a mirror-image position. Sew together exactly on the drawn line. Press and trim, referring to "Pressing Triangle Units" on page 13. Repeat for a total of 88 light green point units and 40 medium green point units.

Make 88
light.

Make 40
medium.

9. Join a light green point unit to opposite sides of a light green nine-patch unit. Press the seam allowances toward the block center. Repeat for a total of 22 light green pieced nine-patch units and 10 medium green pieced nine-patch units.

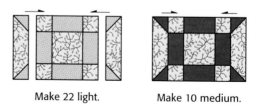

Make 22 light.

Make 10 medium.

10. Join a 1½" tan print square to each end of the remaining light and medium green point units. Press the seam allowances toward the tan print. Join these pieced point units to the remaining sides of the nine-patch units for a total of 22 light green Star blocks and ten medium green Star blocks. Press the seam allowances toward the block centers. The pieced Star blocks should now measure 6½" square.

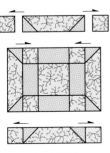 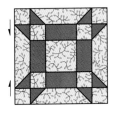

Make 22 light.   Make 10 medium.

ASSEMBLE THE QUILT CENTER

1. Using the quilt photo as a guide, lay out 32 Framed Nine Patch blocks and 32 Star blocks in alternating positions to form eight horizontal rows of eight blocks each. Join the blocks in each row and press the seam allowances toward the Framed Nine Patch blocks. Then join the rows and press the seam allowances in one direction.

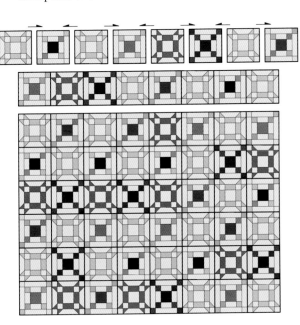

2. Join a 1½" x 48½" tan print strip to the right and left sides of the quilt center. Press the seam allowances toward the tan print. Join a 1½" x 50½" tan print strip to the remaining sides of the quilt center. Press the seam allowances toward the tan print. The pieced quilt center should now measure 50½" square.

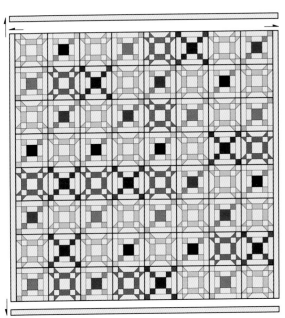

PIECE AND ADD THE INNER BORDERS

1. Using a mechanical pencil, lightly draw a diagonal line on the wrong side of the remaining 1½" light green print squares.

2. With right sides together, layer a prepared 1½" green print square over one corner of a 2½" tan print square. Sew together exactly on the drawn line. Press and trim, referring to "Pressing Triangle Units" on page 13. In the same manner, sew, press, and trim the opposite corner. Then sew the two remaining corners. Repeat for a total of 104 light green Square-in-a-Square blocks measuring 2½" square.

Make 104.

3. Join 25 Square-in-a-Square blocks to form a border strip. Press the seam allowances open. Repeat for a total of two border strips. Join these strips to the right and left sides of the quilt center. Press the seam allowances toward the quilt center. In the same manner, use 27 Square-in-a-Square blocks to form a third and fourth border strip. Join them to the remaining sides of the quilt top. The quilt top should now measure 54½" square.

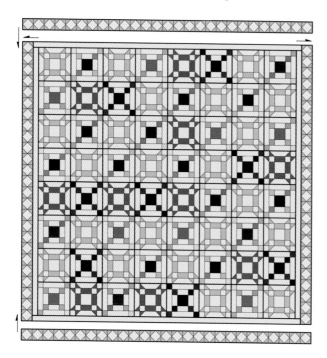

APPLIQUÉ THE MIDDLE BORDERS

Referring to the "Machine Appliqué Made Easy" section on pages 21–24, prepare the appliqués. Please note that for each rose you will use two pieces made with pattern A, one piece made with pattern B, and one piece made with pattern C.

1. With *wrong* sides together, fold each 1½" x 18" light green print strip in half lengthwise and stitch a scant ¼" in from the long raw edges to form a tube. Insert the bias bar into the tube and slide it along as you press the stem, making sure the seam is centered and lies flat.

Bias bar

2. With right sides together, fold the 7½" x 54½" tan print strips in half crosswise and use an iron on a dry setting to lightly press a valley crease. Refold the strips in half lengthwise and press a valley crease through the length of each. Repeat with the 7½" x 68½" tan print strips.

Center

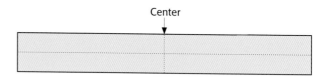

3. Beginning at the center, measure out 9" along the lengthwise crease. Measure 1½" out to each side of this position and mark the location with a small pencil dot. Repeat with the remaining border strips.

4. Beginning at the center point of a border strip, use a fabric glue stick to affix the stem to the background, working from the middle of the stem out and curving it gently away from the center of the border until the inner edge of the stem tip rests on the pencil dot. Repeat with the remaining side of the stem. Add a second stem in a mirror-image position. Repeat this process with the remaining border strips.

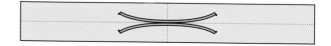

5. Referring to "Invisible Machine Appliqué" on pages 24–26, appliqué the affixed stems to the borders. Using the quilt photo as a guide and working from the bottom layer to the top, add the rose and leaf appliqués to the existing vines.

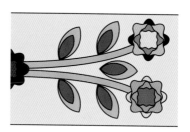

ADD THE APPLIQUÉ BORDERS

1. Join a 54½" appliquéd border strip to the right and left sides of the quilt top. Press the seam allowances toward the border strips. Join a 68½" appliquéd border strip to the remaining sides of the quilt top. Press the seam allowances toward the border strips.

2. Cut the remaining 18" stems in half. Find the position at each border corner where the center creases intersect and mark it with a pencil dot. Use this position to lay out and appliqué the remaining stems and roses as instructed in "Appliqué the Middle Borders" on page 108.

PIECE AND ADD THE OUTER BORDERS

1. Using a mechanical pencil, lightly draw a diagonal line on the wrong side of the remaining 1½" medium green print squares.

2. Referring to step 2, "Piece and Add the Inner Borders" on page 107, make a total of 140 medium green print Square-in-a-Square blocks.

3. Join 34 medium green Square-in-a-Square blocks and press the seam allowances open. Repeat for a total of two border strips. Join these strips to the right and left sides of the quilt top. Press the seam allowances toward the middle border. In the same manner, make two border strips using 36 medium green Square-in-a-Square blocks. Join these strips to the remaining sides of the quilt top. Press the

seam allowances toward the middle border. The finished quilt top should now measure 72½" square.

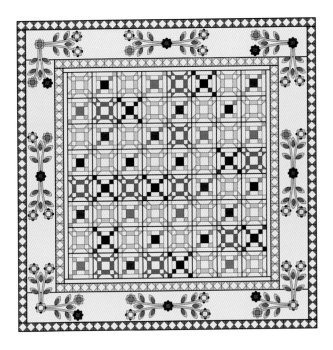

COMPLETE THE QUILT

Refer to "Finishing Techniques" on pages 16–20 for details as needed. Layer the quilt top, batting, and backing. Quilt the layers together. The featured quilt was machine quilted with small feathered plumes radiating out from the center of the Star blocks, and a free-form floral design centered over each Framed Nine Patch block. The border was echo quilted to emphasize the appliqués. Use the eight 2½" x 42" medium green print strips to bind the quilt.

FLOOR PILLOW

Finished Floor Pillow Size: 34½" x 34½"

Designed by Kim Diehl. Pieced and machine
appliquéd by Terry Anderson. Machine quilted
by Kathy Ockerman.

MATERIALS FOR FLOOR PILLOW

Yardages are based on 42"-wide fabric.
- 1⅝ yards of tan print for background
- 1 yard of medium green print for appliqués, border, and binding
- ¾ yard of light green print for appliqués and border
- Scraps of assorted gold, cranberry, plum, and salmon print for appliqués
- 40" x 40" square of muslin for quilt backing
- 1⅜ yards of fabric for backing
- 40" x 40" square of batting
- ⅜" bias bar
- 27" square pillow form

CUTTING

All strips are cut across the width of the fabric unless otherwise noted. Refer to page 113 for the appliqué pattern pieces.

From the light green print, cut:
- 10 strips, 1½" x 42"; crosscut into 192 squares, 1½" x 1½", and 4 strips, 1½" x 20"
- 20 pattern D pieces

From the tan print, cut:
- 1 square, 22½" x 22½"
- 11 strips, 2½" x 42"; crosscut into 112 squares, 2½" x 2½"; 2 strips, 2½" x 26½"; and 2 strips, 2½" x 30½"

From the medium green print, cut:
- 10 strips, 1½" x 42"; crosscut into 256 squares, 1½" x 1½"
- 4 strips, 2½" x 42"
- 20 pattern E pieces

From the assorted gold print scraps, cut:
- 4 pattern A pieces
- 2 pattern B pieces
- 2 pattern C pieces

From the assorted cranberry print scraps, cut:
- 6 pattern A pieces
- 3 pattern B pieces
- 3 pattern C pieces

From the assorted plum print scraps, cut:
- 4 pattern A pieces
- 2 pattern B pieces
- 2 pattern C pieces

From the assorted salmon print scraps, cut:
- 4 pattern A pieces
- 2 pattern B pieces
- 2 pattern C pieces

From the backing fabric, cut:
- 2 rectangles, 25" x 34½"
- 3 strips, 2" x 24"

Appliqué the Pillow Center

Referring to "Machine Appliqué Made Easy" on pages 21–24, prepare the appliqués.

1. Referring to step 1 of "Appliqué the Middle Borders" on page 108, prepare four 20" stems using the 1½" x 20" light green print strips.

2. With right sides together, fold and press a light crease vertically, horizontally, and diagonally into the 22½" tan print square.

3. Referring to "Invisible Machine Appliqué" on pages 24–26 and using the pillow photo and pressed creases as a guide, position the stems on the background square; appliqué in place.

4. Lay out and appliqué the remaining pattern pieces to the background, working from the bottom layer to the top.

Piece and Add the Borders

1. Using a mechanical pencil, lightly draw a diagonal line on the reverse of the 192 light green 1½" squares and the 256 medium green 1½" squares.

2. Referring to step 2 of "Piece and Add the Inner Borders" on page 107, make 48 light green and tan Square-in-a-Square blocks and 64 medium green and tan Square-in-a-Square blocks.

3. Sew 11 light green Square-in-a-Square blocks together to make two inner-border strips. Press the seam allowances open. Join these strips to the right and left sides of the center square. Press the seam allowances toward the center square. In the same manner, use 13 light green Square-in-a-Square blocks to make a third and fourth inner-border strip. Join these strips to the remaining sides of the center square and press the seam allowance toward the center square.

4. Join a 2½" x 26½" tan print strip to the right and left sides of the pillow top. Press the seam allowances toward the tan print strip. Join a 2½" x 30½" tan print strip to the remaining sides of the pillow top. Press the seam allowances toward the tan print.

5. Use 15 medium green print Square-in-a-Square blocks to make two outer-border strips as instructed previously in step 3. Join the strips to the right and left sides of the pillow top. Press the seam allowances toward the tan print. In the same manner, use 17 medium green print Square-in-a-Square blocks to form two more outer-border strips. Join the strips to the remaining sides of the pillow top. Press the seam allowance toward the tan print. The pillow top should now measure 34½" square.

Quilt the Pillow Top

Refer to "Finishing Techniques" on pages 16–20 for details as needed. Layer the pillow top, batting, and muslin backing. Quilt the layers together. The background of the featured pillow was echo quilted to emphasize the appliqués.

Piece the Pillow Back

1. Use an overcast or zigzag stitch to finish one 34½" side of each of the backing squares. Turn each of those edges under to the back, measuring in 4" from the finished edge, and press the folds.

2. With right sides up, overlap the back pieces at the folds so that the overlapped backing square measures 34½" x 34½". Pin in place and stitch the raw edges of the overlapped cloth together with a ⅛" seam to hold folds in place.

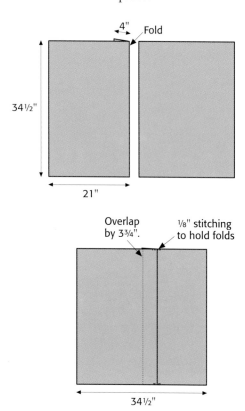

3. Use a bias tape maker to fold and press both long edges of each 2" x 24" strip to the center. Fold the raw edges at each end under ¼" and stitch in place. Fold the strips in half lengthwise to enclose the raw edges, and stitch together along the double-folded edge with a ⅛" seam allowance. Cut each of the sewn ties in half to form six equal pieces.

4. Find the center of the back opening. Sew one tie to each side of the opening, about ½" in from the folded edges, and tuck the raw edges of the ties under to enclose them. Measure out 6" to each side of the center ties, and repeat the process for a total of three sets of ties.

NOTE: A small scrap of cloth or interfacing can be positioned on the wrong side of the pillow backing under the ties for added durability when they are stitched.

ASSEMBLE THE PILLOW

1. Center the quilted pillow front over the pillow back with wrong sides together. Sew around the middle border through all layers, ½" out from the outside edge of the light green Square-in-a-Square border, to form a 27" center to hold the pillow form. This will create a flat flange on the outside of the pillow.

2. Stitch along the outer border, ⅛" in from the raw edges to anchor the pillow front to the back. Slip stitch the folded edges of the back that are enclosed in the flanged border. Trim away any excess batting and backing so that all raw edges are flush with each other.

3. Referring to "Binding" on pages 18–19, use the four 2½" x 42" medium green print strips and a ¼" seam allowance to bind the raw edges. Insert the pillow form.

Appliqué Patterns

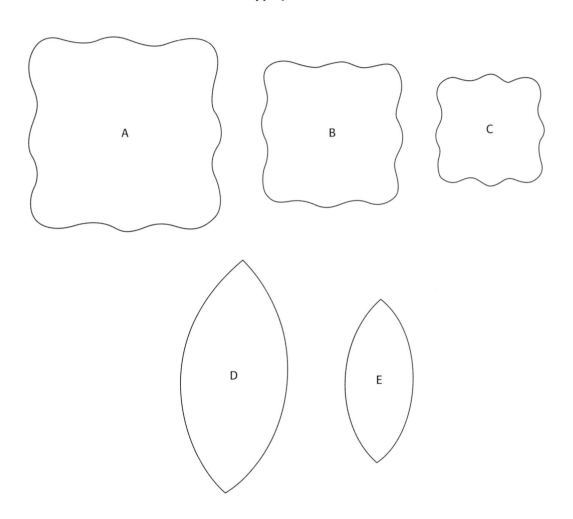

LAZY DAY PLEASURES

Colorful patchwork spools bask in the embrace of twining leafy vines and invite you to do the same! A perfect project for those last remnants you've been saving from your favorite prints.

Finished Quilt Size: 61½" x 61½"

MATERIALS FOR LAP QUILT

Yardages are based on 42"-wide fabric.
- 3⅝ yards of tan print for background
- ⅝ yard of medium green print for vines
- 5 fat quarters of assorted green prints for appliqués
- 100 assorted print scraps for blocks, appliqués, and binding
- 4¼ yards of fabric for backing
- 67" x 67" square of batting
- ⅜" bias bar

CUTTING

All strips are cut across the width of the fabric unless otherwise noted. Refer to page 119 for the appliqué pattern pieces.

From *each* of 100 assorted print scraps, cut:
- 4 squares, 2" x 2"
- 1 rectangle, 2" x 5"

From the tan print, cut:
- 25 strips, 2" x 42"; crosscut into 200 rectangles, 2" x 5"
- 4 strips, 8½" x 68", from the *length* of the fabric

Also from the assorted print scraps, cut:
- A total of 50 rectangles, 2½" x 6", for binding
- 48 pattern B pieces

From the medium green print, cut:
- 10 strips, 1½" x 42"
- 40 pattern A pieces

From *each* of the 5 fat quarters of assorted green prints, cut:
- 40 pattern A pieces

PIECE THE SPOOL BLOCKS

1. Using a mechanical pencil, lightly draw a diagonal line on the wrong side of each 2" assorted print square.

2. With right sides together, layer a prepared 2" square over each end of a 2" x 5" tan print rectangle in a mirror-image position; use 2" squares cut from the same print. Sew together exactly on the drawn lines. Press and trim, referring to

"Pressing Triangle Units" on page 13. Repeat for a total of 200 spool side units—two from each print.

Make 200.

3. Join a spool side unit to each opposite side of a matching print 2" x 5" rectangle. Press the seam allowances toward the center rectangle. Repeat for a total of 100 Spool blocks measuring 5" square.

Make 100.

ASSEMBLE THE QUILT CENTER

Lay out the blocks in alternating positions to form 10 horizontal rows of 10 blocks each. Sew the blocks together in each row. Press the seam allowances toward the tan print. Then join the rows and press the seam allowances in one direction. The pieced quilt center should now measure 45½" square.

ADD AND MITER THE BORDERS

Add and miter the borders, referring to "Mitered Borders" on pages 14–15. Use the tan 8½" x 68" strips.

APPLIQUÉ THE BORDERS

Referring to "Machine Appliqué Made Easy" on pages 21–24, prepare the appliqués.

1. Using a water-soluble marker, draw a line along the length of each border strip, measuring out 4" from the border seams. Do not mark into the corner areas, but start and stop the lines at the edge of the quilt center.

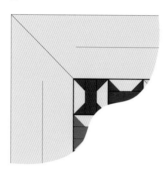

2. Use a dinner plate or the rim of a bowl to draw an arc through the corners and connect the lines.

3. Join five 1½" x 42" medium green print strips end to end to form a vine strip. Press the seam allowances open. With *wrong* sides together, fold the vine strip in half lengthwise and stitch a scant ¼" in from the long raw edges to form a tube. Insert the bias bar into the tube and slide it along as you press the vine, making sure the seam is centered and lies flat.

Bias bar

4. Fold, sew, and press the remaining five 1½" x 42" green strips into five separate lengths of vine as instructed in step 3. Cut each length into 4" segments for a total of 48 stems.

Lazy Day Pleasures Lap Quilt

Finished Quilt Size: 61½" x 61½" • Finished Block Size: 4½"

Designed, pieced, and machine appliquéd by Kim Diehl. Machine quilted by Kathy Ockerman.

5. Fold a pleat 1" in from the end of a 4" stem to form a 90° angle, and secure the fold with a pin. Repeat for a total of 24 folded stems. Prepare the remaining 24 stems in the same manner to form mirror-image folded stems.

Make 24 and 24 reversed.

6. Using the quilt photo as a guide and the drawn lines for placement, position and appliqué the folded stems along the border, referring to "Invisible Machine Appliqué" on pages 24–26. Then add the vines. Please note that the raw edges of the vine were turned under ¼" where they met each other and positioned over a 4" stem to make them less visible.

Begin and end vine.

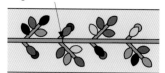

7. Lay out and appliqué the remaining pattern pieces to the border.

COMPLETE THE QUILT

Refer to "Finishing Techniques" on pages 16–20 for details as needed. Layer the quilt top, batting, and backing. Quilt the layers together. The featured quilt was machine quilted in an overall pattern of spiraling circles that resemble cinnamon-roll swirls. Join the assorted print 2½" x 6" rectangles end to end and use them to bind the quilt.

Appliqué Patterns

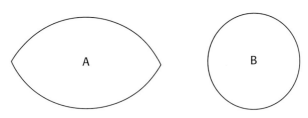

BASKETS OF BLOOMERS

Reap what you sew when you fashion these little garden baskets brimming over with an enticing array of fabric bloomers.

Finished Wall-Hanging Size: 50½" x 53½"

MATERIALS FOR WALL HANGING

Yardages are based on 42"-wide fabric.
- 1⅞ yards of cranberry print for outer border and binding
- 9 fat quarters of assorted neutral background prints for blocks and sashing
- 9 fat eighths of assorted dark tan prints for basket bases
- Approximately 1¼ yards *total* of assorted print scraps for appliqués and sashing
- 3½ yards of fabric for backing
- 56" x 59" piece of batting

CUTTING

All strips are cut across the width of the fabric unless otherwise noted. Refer to pages 127–135 for the appliqué pattern pieces.

Basket Blocks

From *each* of the 9 assorted neutral background prints, cut:
- 2 rectangles, 2½" x 3½"
- 2 rectangles, 1½" x 3½"
- 1 rectangle, 5½" x 8½"
- 1 rectangle, 1½" x 8½"

From *each* of the 9 assorted dark tan prints, cut:
- 1 rectangle, 2½" x 6½"
- 1 rectangle, 1½" x 4½"

Sashing Strips and Nine-Patch Corner Post Blocks

From the 9 assorted neutral background prints, cut a combined total of:
- 80 squares, 1½" x 1½"
- 12 rectangles, 1½" x 8½"
- 12 rectangles 1½" x 9½"

From the assorted print scraps, cut a combined total of:
- 64 squares, 1½" x 1½"
- 24 rectangles, 1½" x 8½"
- 24 rectangles, 1½" x 9½"

Inner Border

From the 9 assorted neutral background prints, cut:
- Enough random lengths of 1½"-wide strips to make two 39½" long strips when joined end to end
- Enough random lengths of 1½"-wide strips to make two 38½" long strips when joined end to end

Outer Border and Binding

From the cranberry print, cut:

- 1 strip, 2½" x 42"; crosscut into 16 squares, 2½" x 2½"
- 6 strips, 2½" x 42", for binding
- 2 strips, 6½" x 38½", from the length of the fabric
- 2 strips, 6½" x 41½", from the length of the fabric

From the 9 assorted neutral prints, cut a combined total of:

- 20 squares, 2½" x 2½"

PIECE THE BASES FOR THE BASKET BLOCKS

1. Align the ends of two 2½" x 3½" neutral print rectangles with opposite ends of a 2½" x 6½" dark tan print rectangle. With a mechanical pencil, lightly draw a diagonal line on each neutral rectangle in mirror-image positions, beginning at the top inner point and ending directly over the outside corner of the dark tan print rectangle positioned underneath. Pin in place and sew together exactly on the drawn lines. Press and trim, referring to "Pressing Triangle Units" on page 13 and directing the seam allowance toward the neutral print.

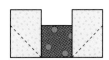 

2. Join two 1½" x 3½" neutral print rectangles to a 1½" x 4½" dark tan print rectangle in the same manner as instructed in step 1.

3. Lay out the pieced units formed in steps 1 and 2 with a 5½" x 8½" neutral print rectangle to form the base for the Basket block. Join the rows, taking care to leave openings along the top sides of the basket where needed for the appliqués. Press the seam allowances toward the dark tan print.

4. Join a 1½" x 8½" neutral print rectangle to the bottom of the block. Press the seam allowances toward the neutral rectangle.

5. Repeat steps 1 through 4 for a total of nine bases for the Basket blocks measuring 8½" x 9½".

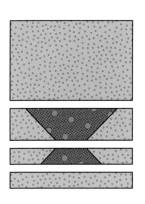
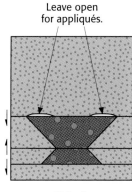

Leave open for appliqués.

Make 9.

APPLIQUÉ THE BASKET BLOCKS

To simplify the appliqué process, the patterns for each block are numbered according to their degree of difficulty, with number 9 being the most challenging. Referring to "Machine Appliqué Made Easy" on pages 21–24, trace and prepare the appliqués from the patterns provided on pages 127–135. Lay out and stitch the appliqués to the block bases, working from the bottom layer to the top and referring to "Invisible Machine Appliqué" on pages 24–26.

PIECE THE SASHING STRIPS AND NINE-PATCH CORNER POST BLOCKS

1. Lay out five 1½" neutral print squares and four 1½" assorted print squares in three horizontal rows to form a Nine-Patch Corner Post block. Sew together the pieces in each row and press the seam allowances toward the dark print. Join the rows and press the seam allowances toward the center row. Repeat for a total of 16 Nine-Patch Corner Post blocks measuring 3½" square.

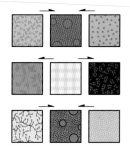 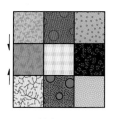

Make 16.

Basket of Bloomers Wall Hanging

Finished Wall-Hanging Size: 50½" x 53½" • Finished Block Size: 8" x 9"

Designed, pieced, and machine appliquéd by Kim Diehl. Hand quilted by Kim Diehl
with machine quilting by Kathy Ockerman.

2. Join a 1½" x 8½" assorted print rectangle to each long side of a 1½" x 8½" neutral print rectangle. Press the seam allowances toward the dark print. Repeat for a total of 12 pieced horizontal sashing-strip segments measuring 3½" x 8½".

Make 12.

3. Join a 1½" x 9½" assorted print rectangle to each long side of a 1½" x 9½" neutral print rectangle. Press the seam allowances toward the dark print. Repeat for a total of 12 pieced vertical sashing-strip segments measuring 3½" x 9½".

Make 12.

PIECE THE WALL-HANGING CENTER

Using the illustration below as a guide, lay out the nine Basket blocks, 16 Nine-Patch Corner Post blocks, 12 horizontal sashing-strip segments, and the 12 vertical sashing-strip segments to form the quilt center. Join the pieces in each horizontal row and press the seam allowances toward the sashing-strip segments. Then join the rows. Press the seam allowances toward the sashing-strip segments. The pieced wall-hanging center should now measure 36½" x 39½".

PIECE AND ADD THE INNER BORDER

1. Sew the random lengths of 1½"-wide neutral strips together end to end to form two 39½" long strips and two 38½" long strips. Press the seam allowances in one direction.

2. Join a 39½" pieced strip to the right and left sides of the wall-hanging center. Press the seam allowances toward the neutral print strips. Join the 38½" strips to each end of the wall-hanging center and press the seam allowances toward the neutral print strips.

ADD THE OUTER BORDER

1. Lay out the five 2½" neutral print squares and four 2½" cranberry print squares in three rows to form a Nine Patch block. Sew and press as instructed in step 1 of "Piece the Sashing Strips and Nine-Patch Corner Post Blocks." Repeat for a total of four Nine Patch blocks measuring 6½" square.

2. Join a 6½" x 41½" cranberry print strip to the right and left sides of the quilt top. Press the seam allowances toward the cranberry print.

3. Join a Nine Patch block to each end of the 38½" cranberry print strips. Press the seam allowances toward the cranberry print.

4. Join the strips pieced in step 3 to the top and bottom of the quilt top. Press the seam allowances toward the cranberry print. The finished quilt top should now measure 50½" x 53½".

COMPLETE THE WALL HANGING

Refer to "Finishing Techniques" on pages 16–20 for details as needed. Layer the wall-hanging top, batting, and backing. Quilt the layers together. The featured wall hanging was hand quilted in the blocks to outline the appliqué shapes, with a cross hatch placed in the basket bases. The border was machine quilted with a feathered cable interspersed with curved leaves. Join the six 2½" x 42" cranberry print strips end to end and bind the wall hanging.

Appliqué Patterns
Block 1: Tulips

Note: Basket is shown for placement purposes only.

Appliqué Patterns
Block 2: Gerbera Daisies

*Note: Basket is shown for placement purposes only.
The dashed lines on the leaves denote
placement of the pattern piece on the seam line
of two joined prints, which is optional.*

Appliqué Patterns
Block 3: Pomegranates

Note: Basket is shown for placement purposes only.

Appliqué Patterns

Block 4: Hollyhocks

Note: Basket is shown for placement purposes only.

Appliqué Patterns
Block 5: Marigolds

Note: Basket is shown for placement purposes only.

Appliqué Patterns
Block 6: Black-Eyed Susans

*Note: Basket is shown for placement purposes only.
The dashed lines on the leaves denote
placement of the pattern piece on the seam line
of two joined prints, which is optional.*

Note: Basket is shown for placement purposes only.

Appliqué Patterns
Block 8: Cabbage Rose

Note: Basket is shown for placement purposes only.

Appliqué Patterns
Block 9: Berries

Note: Basket is shown for placement purposes only.

BLOSSOM BRAMBLE

Create a bramble of pieced posies for your bed with this soft and winsome quilt. Then let the array of prints and colors inspire your choices for coordinating accessories.

Finished Quilt Size: 104½" x 101½"

MATERIALS FOR BED QUILT

Yardages are based on 42"-wide fabric.
- 12⅛ yards of tan print for background and binding
- 2⅛ yards of green print for patchwork and stems
- 2 yards of assorted prints for blocks
- 9 yards of fabric for backing (3 widths pieced lengthwise)
- 110" x 107" piece of quilt backing
- ⅜" bias bar

CUTTING

All strips are cut across the width of the fabric unless otherwise indicated.

From the green print, cut:
- 8 strips, 2" x 42"; crosscut into 150 squares, 2" x 2"
- 4 strips, 1⅞" x 42"; crosscut into 75 squares, 1⅞" x 1⅞"
- 12 strips, 1½" x 42"; crosscut into 290 squares, 1½" x 1½"
- 20 strips, 1¼" x 42"

From each of the assorted prints, cut:
- 1 square, 2½" x 2½" (total of 150 for blossom bases)
- 4 squares, 1½" x 1½" (total of 600 for flower points)

NOTE: As you may not have 150 different prints, please plan to cut sets of prints that include one 2½" blossom base and four 1½" flower point squares.

From the tan print, cut:
- 101 strips, 1½" x 42"; crosscut into:
  590 rectangles, 1½" x 2½"
  300 squares, 1½" x 1½"
  130 rectangles, 1½" x 12½"
  10 rectangles, 1½" x 11½"
  10 rectangles, 1½" x 6½"
  10 rectangles, 1½" x 5½"
- 15 strips, 2½" x 42"; crosscut into 160 rectangles, 2½" x 3½"
- 4 strips, 1⅞" x 42"; crosscut into 75 squares, 1⅞" x 1⅞"
- 13 strips, 3½" x 42"; crosscut into 140 squares, 3½" x 3½"
- 4 strips, 6½" x 42"; crosscut into 20 rectangles, 6½" x 7½"
- 12 strips, 2½" x 42"
- 9 strips, 3" x 101½", from the *length* of the fabric
- 2 strips, 6½" x 101½", from the *length* of the fabric

PIECE THE BLOSSOM BLOCKS

1. Using a mechanical pencil, lightly draw a diagonal line on the wrong side of each 2" green print square.

Pin Point

For patchwork projects containing small-scale pieces, reduce the length of your machine stitches slightly to achieve more stitches to the inch. Your seams will be more secure and the threads in your seams less visible.

2. With right sides together, layer a prepared 2" green print square over one corner of a 2½" assorted print square. Sew together exactly on the drawn line. Press and trim, referring to "Pressing Triangle Units" on page 13. Repeat for a total of 150 blossom bases.

Make 150.

3. Using a mechanical pencil, lightly draw a diagonal line on the wrong side of each 1½" assorted print square.

4. With right sides together, layer a prepared 1½" assorted print square over one end of a 1½" x 2½" tan print rectangle. Sew together exactly on the drawn line. Press and trim, referring to "Pressing Triangle Units" on page 13.

5. Layer a prepared 1½" square of the same print on the opposite end of a pieced rectangle in a mirror-image position. Sew, press, and trim as instructed in step 4. Repeat for a total of 300 blossom point units, two from each assorted print.

Make 300.

6. With right sides together, join a blossom point unit to one side of a matching print blossom base. Press the seam allowance toward the blossom base. Repeat for a total of 150 block units.

Make 150.

7. With right sides together, join a 1½" tan print square to one side of each remaining blossom point unit. Press the seam allowance toward the tan print. Join this pieced unit to the adjacent side of a matching blossom base. Press the seam allowance toward the blossom base. Repeat for a total of 150 Blossom blocks measuring 3½" square.

Make 150.

PIECE THE BLOCK UNITS

1. With right sides together, join a 2½" x 3½" tan print rectangle to one side of a Blossom block. Press the seam allowance toward the tan print. Repeat for a total of 80 blossom units. Make 70 mirror-image units in the same manner.

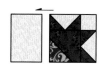

Make 80. Make 70 mirror-image.

2. Using a mechanical pencil, lightly draw a diagonal line on the wrong side of the 1⅞" tan print squares.

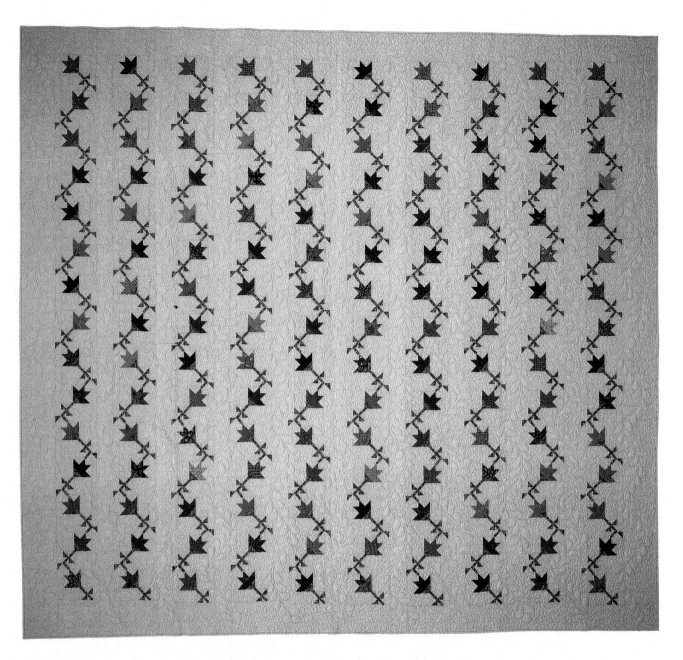

Blossom Bramble Bed Quilt

Finished Quilt Size: 104½" x 101½" • Finished Block Size: 3"

Designed, pieced, and machine appliquéd by Kim Diehl.
Machine quilted by Celeste Freiberg and Kathy Ockerman.

3. With right sides together, layer together a 1⅞" prepared tan print with a 1⅞" green print square. Sew together ¼" out from each side of the drawn line. Cut the pair apart on the drawn line. Press the seam allowances toward the green print. Repeat for a total of 150 half-square-triangle units.

Make 150.

4. Prepare the 290 green print 1½" squares as instructed in step 2.

5. With right sides together, layer a prepared green print square over one end of a 1½" x 2½" tan print rectangle. Sew together exactly on the drawn line. Press and trim, referring to "Pressing Triangle Units" on page 13. Repeat for a total of 80 pieced rectangles. Make 70 mirror-image pieced rectangles in the same manner.

Make 80.   Make 70 mirror image.

6. Join the green side of a 1½" half-square-triangle unit to a 1½" tan print square. Press the seam allowances toward the tan print. Repeat for a total of 80 pieced units. Make 70 mirror-image pieced units in the same manner.

Make 80.   Make 70 mirror image.

7. Join a pieced rectangle formed in step 5 to a unit formed in step 6. Press the seam allowances toward the pieced rectangle. Repeat for a total of 80 leaf units. Make 70 mirror-image leaf units in the same manner.

Make 80.   Make 70 mirror image.

8. Join a 1½" x 2½" tan print rectangle to the bottom of 70 leaf units, and the 70 mirror-image leaf units. Press the seam allowances toward the tan print. Reserve the remaining 10 leaf units.

Make 70.   Make 70 mirror image.

9. Join a 3½" tan print square to the left side of 70 leaf units. Press the seam allowances toward the tan print. Make 70 pieced mirror-image leaf units in the same manner.

Make 70.   Make 70 mirror image.

10. Join a pieced leaf unit from step 9 to the bottom of a blossom unit. Press the seam allowance toward the leaf unit. Repeat for a total of 70 blossom units. Make 70 mirror-image blossom units in the same manner.

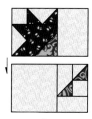 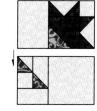

Make 70.   Make 70 mirror image.

11. Join a 2½" x 3½" tan print rectangle to the left side of each reserved leaf unit. Press the seam allowances toward the tan print. Join the pieced leaf units to the remaining blossom units to form 10 row bases. Press seam allowances toward the leaf units.

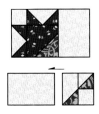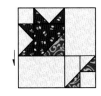

Make 10.

PIECE THE ROWS

1. Lay out seven blossom units and seven mirror-image blossom units in alternating positions to form a vertical row. Please note that the first block should face to the upper left. Add a row base unit to the bottom. Join the pieces and press the seam allowances away from the blossom points. Repeat for a total of 10 rows.

2. Join a 1½" green print square to one end of a 1½" x 12½" tan print strip. Press and trim, referring to "Pressing Triangle Units" on page 13. Repeat for a total of 70 pieced sashing strips. Make 60 mirror-image pieced sashing strips in the same manner.

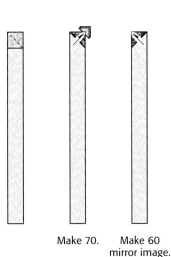

Make 70.　Make 60 mirror image.

3. Sew a prepared 1½" green print square to the end of a 1½" x 6½" tan print rectangle, positioning the green print to make the same mirror-image triangle formed in step 2. Repeat for a total of 10 pieced rectangles.

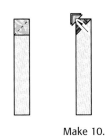

Make 10.

4. Join seven pieced 12½" sashing strips from step 2 end to end to form one pieced row. Be sure that all the green triangles are facing the same direction. Press the seam allowances toward the tan print. Join a 1½" x 5½" tan print rectangle to the top of the row. Press the seam allowance away from the green print. Repeat for a total of 10 pieced sashing rows.

5. Join a pieced sashing row to the right side of each vertical blossom row. Press the seam allowances toward the sashing.

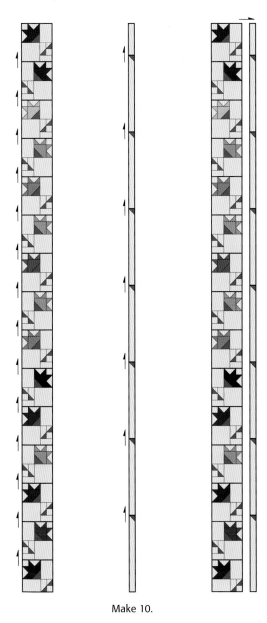

Make 10.

6. Join six mirror-image pieced 12½" sashing strips together end to end to form one pieced row. Press the seam allowances toward the tan print. Join a 1½" x 11½" tan print strip to the top of the row, and a 1½" x 6½" pieced rectangle to the bottom of the row. Press the seam allowances as shown. Repeat for a total of 10 pieced sashing rows.

7. Join a pieced sashing row to the left side of each vertical blossom row. Press the seam allowances toward the sashing.

8. Sew a 6½" x 7½" tan print rectangle to the top and bottom of each row. Press the seam allowances toward the tan print rectangles. The pieced vertical rows should now measure 7½" x 101½".

PREPARE AND APPLIQUÉ THE STEMS

1. With wrong sides together, fold the 1¼" x 42" green print strips in half lengthwise and use a scant ¼" seam allowance to stitch together along the long raw edges to form tubes. Insert the bias bar into each tube and slide it along as you press the stem, making sure the seam is centered and lies flat. Cut the prepared stem lengths into 140 pieces that are 5" long, and 10 pieces that are 3½" long.

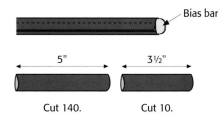

2. Turn under both of the raw ends of a 5" stem a scant ¼", and use a fabric glue stick to anchor them in place. Fold a pleat about 1½" from one end to form a 90° angle and secure the angled fold with a pin. Repeat for a total of 70 folded stems.

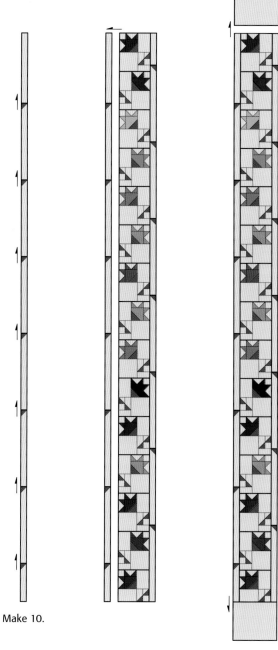

Make 10.

Make 10.

NOTE: After pinning a fold into the first stem, lay it over a block unit to ensure it reaches from just inside the blossom base to the tip of the blossom point below, with the pleat positioned at or near the sashing strip triangle leaf (see detail in step 5 below). Make adjustments if necessary, and then use it as a model to fold the remaining stems.

Make 70 and
70 mirror image.

3. Repeat step 2 to make 70 mirror-image folded stems.

4. Using the quilt photo as a guide, use a fabric glue stick to affix the prepared stems to the rows, leaving the pins in place. Appliqué the stems in place, referring to "Invisible Machine Appliqué" on pages 24–26 and removing the pins as you sew.

5. Affix and appliqué the 3" stems to the bottom of each row, turning under the raw ends as in step 2.

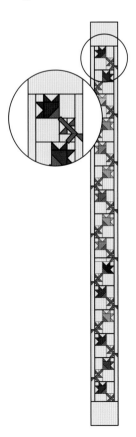

ASSEMBLE THE ROWS

1. Lay out the 10 vertical rows, placing them in alternating positions with the nine tan print strips measuring 3" x 101½". Join the rows. Press the seam allowances toward the tan print strips.

2. Join a 6½" x 101½" tan print strip to the right and left sides of the quilt top. Press the seam allowances toward the tan print strips. The pieced quilt top should now measure 104½" x 101½".

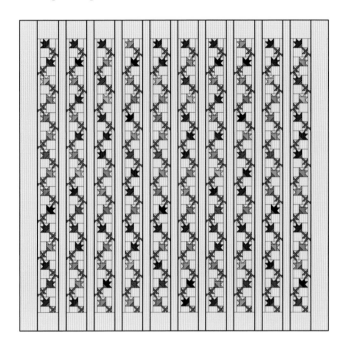

COMPLETE THE QUILT

Refer to "Finishing Techniques" on pages 16–20 for details as needed. Layer the quilt top, batting, and backing. Quilt the layers together. The featured quilt was machine quilted with serpentine feathered cables between each row, and a meandering stipple pattern placed in the open background areas. Use the twelve 2½" x 42" tan print strips to bind the quilt.

ABOUT THE AUTHOR

KIM DIEHL enjoys quiltmaking because of the many challenges and personal rewards it continually brings to her life. Her third quilt was the grand-prize winning entry in *American Patchwork and Quilting* magazine's 1998 "Pieces of the Past" challenge, and since that time she has published numerous original designs in leading quilting magazines. Kim is intrigued by the fact that all quilts are different and yet all quilts are the same, and loves to explore the endless design possibilities that each one presents.

When she is not quilting or teaching her machine appliqué techniques, Kim takes pleasure in antiquing and scouring tag sales for hidden treasures waiting for a second chance to be wonderful. Her favorite summer pasttimes are flower gardening, which she considers a competitive sport, and hand quilting.

Kim, her husband Dan, and their two daughters, Katie and Molly, live in Idaho where they enjoy time spent together at home. Kim is proud to say that both girls have already made their first quilts.